2000

W9-DEI-664
3 0301 00207554 3

Posttenure Faculty Development
Building a System for Faculty Improvement and Appreciation

Jeffrey W. Alstete

ASHE-ERIC Higher Education Report Volume 27, Number 4
Adrianna J. Kezar, Series Editor

Prepared and published by

JOSSEY-BASS
A Wiley Company
San Francisco

In cooperation with

ERIC Clearinghouse on Higher Education
The George Washington University
URL: www.eriche.org

Association for the Study
of Higher Education
URL: http://www.tiger.coe.missouri.edu/~ashe

Graduate School of Education and Human Development
The George Washington University
URL: www.gwu.edu

LIBRARY
UNIVERSITY OF ST. FRANCIS
JOLIET, ILLINOIS

Posttenure Faculty Development: Building a System for
Faculty Improvement and Appreciation
Jeffrey W. Alstete (au.)
ASHE-ERIC Higher Education Report Volume 27, Number 4
Adrianna J. Kezar, Series Editor

This publication was prepared partially with funding from the
Office of Educational Research and Improvement, U.S.
Department of Education, under contract no. ED-99-00-0036.
The opinions expressed in this report do not necessarily re-
flect the positions or policies of OERI or the Department.

Copyright © 2000 Jossey-Bass, a Wiley company. All rights
reserved. Reproduction or translation of any part of this
work beyond that permitted by Sections 107 or 108 of the
1976 United States Copyright Act without permission of the
copyright owner is unlawful. Requests for permission or
further information should be addressed to the Permissions
Department, John Wiley & Sons, Inc., 605 Third Avenue,
New York, NY 10158-0012; (212) 850-6011, fax (212) 850-
6008, e-mail: permreq@wiley.com.

ISSN 0884-0040   ISBN 0-7879-5572-8

The ASHE-ERIC Higher Education Report is part of the
Jossey-Bass Higher and Adult Education Series and is pub-
lished eight times a year by Jossey-Bass, 350 Sansome Street,
San Francisco, California 94104-1342.

For subscription information, see the Back Issue/
Subscription Order Form in the back of this journal.

Prospective authors are strongly encouraged to contact
Adrianna Kezar, Director, ERIC Clearinghouse on Higher
Education, at (202) 296-2597 ext. 14 or akezar@eric-he-edu.

Visit the Jossey-Bass Web site at www.josseybass.com.

Printed in the United States of America on acid-free recycled
paper containing 100 percent recovered waste paper, of
which at least 20 percent is postconsumer waste.

378.122
A463
EXECUTIVE SUMMARY

Despite the continuing changes in higher education and an increasing number of alternatives to tenure today, tenured faculty are the largest cohort of faculty in colleges and universities. The U.S. Department of Education, in a national study of postsecondary faculty (National Center for Education Statistics, 1993), found that 92.8% of all institutional types award tenure and that 51.3% of all faculty were tenured or on a tenure track. The uncapping of the mandatory retirement age, the still widespread awarding of tenure, and the prolonged life span of the professoriat have all combined to increase the number of tenured faculty. This situation is of concern as a variety of external forces affect higher education, including increased use of information technology, globalization of the curriculum, decreasing government support, changing accreditation requirements, continued diversification in student demographics, and negative public perceptions about the tenure system. What will happen as these external influences affect changes in the institutional missions and how the outcomes from higher education are evaluated? The answer could be a negative confrontation as a result of the increasing age and knowledge gap, or a positive learning experience for both generations. Posttenure faculty development is one way to address this challenge.

What Is Faculty Development Today?
Several definitions of faculty development are found in the literature. "Faculty development" is a phrase that has both a broad and a narrow definition. Broadly, it covers a wide range of activities that have as their overall goal the improvement of student learning. More narrowly, the phrase is aimed at helping faculty members improve their competence as teachers and scholars (Eble and McKeachie, 1985). Faculty development programs vary in their purpose, but they are commonly designed to enhance personal and professional development, instructional development, and/or organizational development. Professional development involves promoting faculty growth and enabling faculty members to obtain and enhance job-related skills, knowledge, and awareness. Instructional development involves the preparation of learning materials, styles of instruction, and updating courses. Organizational development focuses on creating an effective institutional atmosphere in which

faculty and faculty development personnel can implement new practices for teaching and learning (Gaff, 1975). Personal development efforts involve a more holistic approach to help faculty members enhance interpersonal skills, promote wellness, and assist with career planning (Graf, Albright, and Wheeler, 1992). Curriculum development is another component that overlaps with each of the preceding areas; it involves the development of additional scholarly and teaching competencies, creation of new instructional materials, and the development of new communication and organizational patterns (Bergquist and Phillips, 1975; Eble and McKeachie, 1985). Based on these definitions, posttenure faculty development involves those activities that seek to improve student learning, teaching, scholarship, and service in higher education by developing personal, instructional, organizational, and curricular aspects of faculty members who have earned tenure.

What Types of Posttenure Faculty Development Programs Have Been Established?

Posttenure faculty development can be classified as optional, required, or jointly sponsored by several institutions. Optional programs can be stand-alone programs or part of a comprehensive faculty development system at an institution. Optional strategies include award programs specifically designed to encourage and motivate tenured faculty, fellowship programs, teaching projects, writing projects, teaching partnerships, workshops, seminars, and development plans. Faculty development plans can be optional or required of all faculty, and methods are available to help motivate tenured faculty for full participation in this process and reward them accordingly. Optional programs have had positive outcomes, including increased faculty performance and student retention, at several institutions.

Required posttenure faculty development is usually part of a formal posttenure review system. Such systems are becoming more common today as the public calls for increased accountability and performance from postsecondary faculty (Licata and Morreale, 1997). This approach has the advantage of institution-supported consequences for nonperformance by the tenured faculty. The development component can be required in all reviews or "triggered" by specific outcomes of a faculty member's evaluation. The development process in these cases normally involves the creation of a faculty development plan, which usually includes specific objectives for teaching, research, and service in a stated time period, along with a follow-up mechanism to ensure performance. The American Association of University Professors (1997) recently issued a statement admitting that posttenure review is becoming a reality and that such systems should be designed to support professional development of and responsibility by the faculty in their duties.

A comprehensive posttenure faculty development program can require a significant institutional investment, but one institution is not required to fund the entire program. Jointly sponsored programs, perhaps cosponsored with other institutions or professional associations, can be effective and relatively low cost.

How Can Development Strategies Be Designed to Improve and Appreciate Tenured Faculty?

Faculty development strategies differ according to institutional type and stated mission. Faculty development programs are more successful if they seek out participation and input from a variety of faculty members (including tenured professors) and consult them in planning decisions (Nelson and Siegel, 1980; Sorcinelli, 1988). Administrators and faculty leaders should clearly define the objectives of the program and what kinds of development (professional, instructional, curricular, organizational) will be emphasized. Department chairs are also a key component of effective faculty development because they are on the front line in handling faculty development plans, travel approvals, course evaluations, and complaints from students. In planning programs, faculty developers should study all aspects of the institution, including its culture, academic programs, committee systems, administrative hierarchy, and organizational structure; they should seek support from the administration. It can be helpful to map out development activities for faculty at different stages of their careers using a template to ensure that the multiple roles faculty must perform are supported. After reviewing the literature, collecting information on process and outcomes from institutions, and reading discussions about these issues, this author recommends that a comprehensive posttenure faculty development system not be formally linked to a posttenure review process so as to separate the evaluative and development components, helping to ensure more effective participation and allowing faculty to set higher achievement goals. An overall model of development programs for tenured faculty should consider the institution's mission, and should consist of optional, jointly sponsored, and required components. Once development plans for tenured faculty are implemented, proper supervision and evaluation are important to continuously improve and maintain quality. One method of accomplishing it is benchmarking, which analyzes institutional faculty development practices and outcomes with selected peers to determine the best practices and potential areas for improvement in an institution.

What Are the Implications of Choosing to Develop Tenured Faculty?

Some view tenure as one of the potential weaknesses that tradition-bound institutions like colleges and universities must overcome. Instead of eliminating tenure as some institutions are doing, creating and implementing development strategies that enable faculty to improve and feel appreciated is a more viable choice. Research has shown that tenured faculty members have many strengths compared with their junior colleagues and that they are more likely to participate in faculty development programs. Whether an institution chooses to implement a required development component as part of a posttenure review system, a series of optional programs, or some combination, it is important that the strategy go beyond a one-time solution and quick cure.

For some faculty members, however, reasonable efforts at bringing renewal will not be successful. For those individuals—and to help ensure the effective development of those tenured faculty who want to continue to grow and learn—the institution should consider other alternatives. Those institutions with a formal posttenure review process already have the mechanism in place to accomplish the proper weeding or termination of nondeveloping faculty. In some colleges and universities, another alternative is an early retirement or phased-retirement policy. This strategy, in combination with effective administrative leadership that points out other consequences for remaining full time and nonproductive, can help motivate some faculty to make the proper choice.

Posttenure faculty development strategies will continue to grow and change as higher education systems are transformed by new technology; new types of students; and new approaches to college teaching, scholarship, and service. Institutions with effective posttenure faculty development strategies will be better able to compete and thrive than those that do not assist their tenured faculty to continually develop and meet new challenges.

CONTENTS

FOREWORD

It is beyond cliché to discuss the increased calls for accountability in higher education over the last 15 years. Assessment, performance indicators, changes in accreditation, performance funding, Total Quality Management, and many other processes call for higher education to provide evidence of performance. Performance measures are being redefined at more levels each year. And posttenure review of faculty members' performance is one way to hold higher education accountable to its constituents. Many individuals suggest that posttenure review undermines academic freedom and tenure. Others believe posttenure review can enhance faculty performance by ensuring more systematic and comprehensive feedback. And still others argue for posttenure faculty development. But faculty development is often noted as a cliché, meeting all the challenges presented to higher education, whether diversity, technology, or globalization. A palpable tension exists between interpreting posttenure review as a measure of accountability or development.

Looking more deeply at the tensions surrounding posttenure review, the AAUP in 1983 developed a statement suggesting that "periodic formal institutional evaluation of each postprobationary faculty member would bring scant benefit, would incur unacceptable costs, not only in money and time but also in dampening of creativity and of collegial relationships, and would threaten academic freedom."AAUP also objects to posttenure review because the process often suggests that tenured faculty do not already undergo continual evaluation from student evaluations, reviews before appointment to school and university committees and graduate faculties, annual evaluations, performance plans, and so on. The AAUP cautions against the use of posttenure review because "at its most draconian, post-tenure review aims to reopen the question of tenure; at its most benign, it formalizes and systematizes longstanding practices" (AAUP, 1999).

There is more agreement that some posttenure review system, aimed at faculty development rather than accountability, is a needed strategy for improving performance. Jeffrey Alstete is aligned with the AAUP in his emphasis on development rather than accountability and the separation of evaluation and development. Instead of posttenure review, the author recommends posttenure faculty development to strengthen support for tenure. Alstete has many years of experience with the development of a posttenure development program as associate dean in the Hagan School of Business at Iona College in New Rochelle, New York. *Posttenure Faculty Development: Building a System for Faculty Improvement and Appreciation* helps to synthesize the debate around posttenure review and develops a model for faculty development that converges the best principles of posttenure review and long-standing practice of faculty assessment and development. Alstete reviews reasons why posttenure faculty development is needed, including the uncapping of mandatory retirement, changes in student demographics and technology, and globalization. Even if your campus is not considering posttenure faculty development, the arguments in *Posttenure Faculty Development* might make you stop and think. Alstete then reviews higher education's progress addressing this changed environment through existing faculty development models. This discussion provides an argument for why efforts to undertake faculty development need to be reexamined and in many cases realigned.

The most important contribution of *Posttenure Faculty Development* is its extensive review of current posttenure faculty development programs and the development of a classification scheme. As campuses undertake posttenure faculty development, they need to understand the various models and the advantages and disadvantages of each type. Toward this end, Alstete offers a model of the important aspects that need to be considered when devising a posttenure faculty development program based on the research. Alstete summarizes research studies on posttenure faculty development for the reader, bringing together the most recent knowledge on this topic. The result is a blueprint for implementation that acknowledges the way models vary by institutional type, stated mission, and campus culture. An important finding is that posttenure faculty development should not be linked with posttenure review so as to separate the evaluative and developmental components. The detailed appendices provide the reader with examples of model posttenure faculty development processes, examples of organizations to contact, and other benchmark data.

Several other ASHE-ERIC monographs can assist you in your efforts to develop a posttenure faculty development program. *A New Alliance* by Mimi Wolverton describes the way principles from Total Quality Management can be used in the classroom to increase faculty performance. A top-selling monograph, *Collaborative Peer Review* by Larry Keig and Michael Waggoner, examines the way to develop successful peer review to evaluate and assess faculty performance. Gaye Luna and Deborah Cullen provide a helpful overview of mentoring in *Empowering the Faculty*, pointing out this important aspect of development that can be formalized to improve performance. One of the most popular approaches to development is portfolios; John Murray highlights this technique in *Successful Faculty Development and Evaluation*. Last, following a main theme of the renewal of senior faculty, *The Vitality of Senior Faculty Members* by Carole Bland and William Bergquist provides even greater detail on this important policy area. With these resources in hand, faculty and administrators have the tools and strategies to ensure support for faculty across their careers.

Adrianna J. Kezar
Series Editor
ASHE-ERIC Higher Education Reports

ACKNOWLEDGMENTS

I wish to thank Dr. Nicholas J. Beutell, dean of the Hagan School of Business at Iona College, for his support of this research and his ideas for effective faculty development strategies. Some of the literature cited was obtained with the help of Adrienne Franco, from the Ryan Library at Iona College, and Patricia A. Wood, the literature database manager at the ERIC Clearinghouse on Higher Education. I also want to thank Stephanie Chiappa, Tara Feller, Michel Lepeltier, and Carol Shea for their assistance. A special thanks is owed to my editor, Adrianna Kezar, who provided encouragement and helpful advice.

This book is dedicated to my daughter, Jessica.

WHY IS DEVELOPMENT OF TENURED FACULTY A CONCERN?

The average age of faculty members in higher education is rising each year, and senior tenured faculty members are now the largest cohort (Finkelstein, 1993; National Center for Education Statistics, 1993). Moreover, the age of the typical faculty member will continue to rise as a result of the uncapping of the mandatory retirement age, the longer life span of today's professoriat, and tenure. Students are still entering college in large numbers after completing secondary school, and some wonder whether faculty in their 50s, 60s, and beyond have the capability and desire to be productive and effective with all that is happening in this postindustrial, information-driven society. *The Digital Economy: Promise and Peril in the Age of Networked Intelligence* (Tapscott, 1996) asks whether the formal education system can transform itself. Geoffrey Bannister, president of Butler University, answers, "Just wait till the generation of teenage Internet users hit the universities when the average age of tenured professors is 50. Sparks are going to fly!" (Tapscott, 1996, p. 37). Of a dozen themes proposed for the new economy, the first is knowledge (Tapscott, 1996). Information technology enables an economy based on knowledge and a subsequent shift or transformation toward knowledge work. Companies and other institutions are no longer valued because of the physical assets of production, raw materials, and so on: They are valued because of what the employees and managers know. We in higher education have believed this truth about our institutions for a long time, and it is one of the supposed reasons that tenure was created—to help recruit and retain the knowledge (in the minds of faculty) of the college and to provide freedom to advance the frontiers of scholarship.

Faculty can and must be part of the transformation.

Today's [faculty] development questions ask not simply how to improve one faculty member's teaching skills but how to revitalize tenured-in departments as a whole, how to create entirely new career options for faculty, how to reformulate the curriculum to attract new student populations, and how to keep the institution alive and competitive. (Bland and Schmitz, 1988, p. 191)

Development of tenured faculty is linked to competitiveness, but some institutions are more concerned about being competitive than others. Some believe that the top 150 or so institutions do not have to worry about the pressures faced by the bulk of colleges and universities (Breneman, 1997; Frank and Cook, 1995). Tenure, and posttenure faculty development, may take a different form in the top institutions from that in the majority of schools. This report is written largely for the majority of institutions where faculty hiring and faculty development activities are influenced by tuition-driven market competitiveness, faculty salaries, and the overall availability of funding.

Colleges and universities of even modest means can accomplish much to enhance faculty careers without Herculean efforts or enormous expenditures (Schuster, 1990). "The quality of higher education and the ability of colleges and universities . . . to perform their respective missions is inextricably linked to the quality and commitment of the faculty" (p. 3). We in higher education have been neither sufficiently alert to the ever changing circumstances of our instructional staffs nor adequately resourceful about meeting their changing needs for professional development (Schuster, 1990). Not surprisingly, a major review of the literature on faculty development has not been done since the 1970s (Bland and Schmitz, 1988; Smith, 1976; Stordahl, 1981).

This monograph first explores faculty development and its relationship to posttenure evaluation, and then explains how a system for improvement of and appreciation for tenured faculty can be built in this era of continuous improvement and lifelong learning. "The digital economy requires a far-reaching rethinking of education and, more broadly, learning and the relationship [among] working, learning, and daily life as a consumer" (Tapscott, 1996, p. 197). Increasingly, work and learning are becoming the same thing in many corporations. Workers and managers are finding that learning has become a lifelong challenge that does not end with a diploma of some type. Private industry has historically relied on colleges and universities for training, but learning is now shifting away from the traditional school system (Tapscott, 1996). Some institutions of higher and postsecondary education are working hard to reinvent themselves for relevance, but progress is slow. "With tenured professors, teachers threatened by technology, less competition, and teaching traditions dating back centuries, many educational institutions have become mired in the past" (p. 201). Faculty development, especially of posttenure professors, is strongly needed as forces in the external environment such as changing technology and increased competition affect higher education. Although faculty development and posttenure review have been topics of significant discussion recently, only a small amount of major work has been done linking these two different yet related concepts (Rifkin, 1995).

Tenured Faculty

The issue of how to supervise faculty effectively has been debated for many years. In 1878, a Cornell University trustee argued for the right of the Cornell board "to dismiss faculty as summarily as businessmen might dismiss factory laborers" (Rudolph, 1977, p. 415). It is not surprising that the early part of the 20th century saw the development of academic tenure and greater professionalism among faculty to help ensure job security and their perceived right to academic freedom. Celebrated cases involving academic freedom in the 1890s and early decades of the 20th century reveal how religious unorthodoxy, pacifism, and critical attitudes toward American economic institutions and practices could embroil professors in controversies with boards of trustees and benefactors. In the end, however, the curriculum as an instrument of intellectual training was enhanced. On the negative side, tenure also protected faculty when their time had gone (Rudolph, 1977). Tenure continued to evolve in the early decades of the 20th century and continues to be a very common policy in postsecondary institutions in the United States today. "Almost all research universities (97%) and public four-year colleges (99%) offer tenure. Among private four-year colleges, only 9 percent do not. About 75 percent of all full-time faculty work on campuses with tenure policies" (Chait and Trower, 1997, p. 1). Tenure does indeed prevent the dismissal of faculty as easily as factory laborers. Unfortunately, it also often limits the administration with regard to the occasionally needed expansion and reduction of the workforce as the budget and enrollment change. To control costs and ensure flexibility, some colleges use term contracts to replace tenure track openings for a growing number of professors (Wilson, personal communication, 1995).

But, as Mark Twain might say, despite reports to the contrary, tenure is alive and well. A national study of postsecondary faculty by the U.S. Department of Education reports that 92.8% percent of institutions award tenure and that 51.3% of the faculty at those institutions are tenured or on tenure track (National Center for Education Statistics, 1993). As one familiar with higher education might expect, tenure is more widely held by faculty at 4-year institutions than at 2-year institutions, and at those primarily publicly funded than at those primarily privately funded. Tenure is especially widespread at research universities, doctoral universities, and comprehensive universities. With regard to academic discipline, faculty in areas such as engineering, health sciences, natural sciences, agriculture, and social sciences are especially likely to be tenured. Overall, tenure of full-time instructional faculty remained largely stable over the 15 years from 1980 to 1995 at approximately 64% (National Center for Education Statistics, 1993).

While not all tenured faculty are over 50, the majority are considered senior faculty in institutional rank.

Who are these tenured faculty members? Only 26.8% of faculty younger than the age of 40 are tenured, whereas 55.5% of tenured faculty are 50 to 60 years old and 61.6% of those over 60 have tenure. While not all tenured faculty are over 50, the majority are considered senior faculty in institutional rank. Tenured faculty largely hold the rank of professor (96.1% have tenure) or associate professor (83.3%), and nontenured faculty are largely assistant professors (only 16.7% hold tenure) or instructors (7.1%). A previous ASHE-ERIC Higher Education Report (Bland and Bergquist, 1997) defines senior faculty as full-time, tenured faculty with at least 15 years of experience in higher education who are over the age of 45. This monograph considers posttenure faculty to be primarily associate or full professors over the age of 45.

The typical employment agreement between professors and institutions in the United States today consists of several stages, from the original appointment through tenure:

1. *The initial appointment as instructor or assistant professor for a limited term;*
2. *A probationary period (including the initial appointment) ranging in various institutions from one to seven years or more;*
3. *Promotion to associate professor and advancement to tenure; and*

4. Eventually, in most cases, advancement to full professor.
(Bowen and Schuster, 1986, pp. 233–234)

The appointment is terminated, however, if tenure is denied at the end of the probationary period. It also may be terminated at other times for adequate cause, which includes discontinuance of a program, neglect of duty, or the institution's financial exigency. The dictionary defines tenure as "permanence of position" or "the holding of something, as an office; an occupation" (Davies, 1981, p. 714). It is this permanence of position and perceived lack of ability to dismiss employees that is at the root of the attack on tenure. Several reasons are commonly advanced for eliminating tenure:

1. The economic squeeze that is affecting business, government, and higher education;
2. The demand for accountability and pressures from state legislatures;
3. Misunderstanding about the nature of faculty work;
4. The privilege of economic security; and
5. The increasing inflexibility and rising cost of higher education's primary workforce, the faculty. (Morreale and Licata, 1997)

Aside from the fiscal problems and envy of others associated with tenure, a very real problem also exists with the general performance of some tenured faculty.

When intelligent and decent people do foolish and
cruel things, it seems safe to assume that they are the
victims of institutions that encourage or demand such
behavior. Such I believe to be the case with tenure. It is
a major premise of this work that tenure, and its part-
ner in crime, the Ph.D., have inflicted what may
turn out to be the fatal wounds on higher education.
(Smith, 1990, p. 114)

Some see tenure as the "academic culture's ultimate control mechanism to weed out the idiosyncratic, the creative, and the nonconformist" that is helping to bring about the demise of higher education (Sykes, 1988, p. 258). But these comments and other writings about the need for eliminating tenure often neglect to consider that opportunities are available for working to review and improve tenured faculty, despite the link to academic freedom.

Academic freedom is a relatively old concept and is now considered a long established reason for needing tenure. Its link with the later evolved tenure system is "of more modern vintage," however (Olswang and Fantel, 1980, p. 1). The concept of academic freedom as we know it today is an outgrowth of the 19th century German protection of the university known as *Lehrfreiheit*, or the freedom to teach without interference from ecclesiastical and government influences. The Germans believed that the freedom of teaching and instruction was the distinctive prerogative of the academic profession and an essential condition of any institution that called itself a university (Metzger, 1955). American universities found this concept of academic freedom in jeopardy in at least three periods in the last 50 years (Woodward, 1997). The first was in the 1940s and 1950s during the hunt for communists, later led by Senator Joseph McCarthy. In response to pressure from the public in the press and church, politicians used the government and legislation to drive many left-leaning scholars from their universities or from higher education entirely. The second attack on academic freedom in colleges came in the 1960s and 1970s, this time not from the right wing of the political spectrum, but from the left. Where the earlier movement used the courts, the law, the subpoena, and the legislative and executive branches of state and federal governments, these student leftists did not. The "movement" involved a vocal minority of student "activists" who resorted to violent confrontations, demonstrations, sit-ins, occupation of academic buildings and administrative offices, trashing of library stacks and catalogs, disruption of classes, and even the taking of senior campus administrators as hostages. Today, the greatest threat to academic freedom comes not from the government or students, but from within (Horn, 1998; Martin and Neal, 1997). The threat today to academic freedom and tenure arises from the beliefs of many faculty and administrators in higher education that the purpose of education is to induce correct opinion rather than to search for wisdom and liberate the mind.

As mentioned, the effects of the internal and external threats to tenure have even resulted in some institutions' developing alternatives to tenure. A recent report describes 43 institutions without tenure and lists their rankings in magazines, salary levels, contractual provisions, policies, and faculty reactions (Chait and Trower, 1997). These contracts have attracted national attention (Wilson, personal communication, 1995), and the lessons learned from contract systems have implications for conventional tenure, which tenure advocates should understand to argue convincingly for the status quo. A more attractive alternative is a periodic review of tenured faculty as part of a program of faculty development, not as a device for abrogating tenure (Bowen and Schuster, 1986). Indeed, many reasons exist to support tenure.

Despite the threats to tenure and academic freedom from inside and outside academe, a 1993 national study found that faculty with tenure publish more and have more contact with students than those without tenure (Lee, 1995; National Center for Education Statistics, 1993). And although on average their research productivity drops slightly with age, "senior" faculty remain highly productive and shift their focus to higher quality research over quantity (Bland and Bergquist, 1997). Tenured faculty often have a useful network of professional colleagues, strong work values, extensive knowledge of academic institutions, and the ability to handle multiple ongoing projects. Interestingly, a 1995 survey of 1,200 provosts of four-year colleges and universities regarding their campus plans found that 31% of the respondents reported no changes in tenure policies. In addition, 29% already have posttenure review processes in place, and 24% have long-term non-tenure-track appointments (Trower, 1996). It is therefore understandable why many faculty believe "if it ain't broke, don't fix it" about many tenure policies (Tarbox, 1996). Others in higher education have a different view, however:

> *In Adam Smith's day students paid their teachers directly. Since then the academy has come a long way from the market—too long away according to many critics. Tenure is supposed to guarantee academic freedom. One of the freedoms it guarantees is the freedom to retire on the job. Academics will question anyone's right to judge their productivity: Administrators have it in for them, students are too ignorant, their parents only care about finding Jr. a high paying job, and Jr.'s*

potential employers could care less about the finer
things in life—they just want Jr. to be vocationally
competent. Who is to be the judge? It is clear that
without anyone judging, the academy has grown fat
and complacent—to the point that efficacy is being
questioned by the society that it serves. Do we want to
be judged by the hoi polloi or do we want to judge
ourselves? (Ditwiler, 1997, p. 1)

Some of these concerns may even become irrelevant, as
some professors may return to being judged and paid directly by their students through distance learning courses via
the Internet and other telecommunications technology. In
addition, the idea of posttenure review seems an almost
mild answer to the feelings expressed by some about tenure.
A well-planned system of honestly reviewing tenured faculty, with peers and others offering responsible judgment,
properly supported development strategies, and strong re-
course when needed can and is addressing societal concerns
at many institutions without treading on academic freedom.
Even so, the posttenure review component of this strategy
also has its critics.

Posttenure Review: The Elephant in the Room
In 1986, one writer believed that performance evaluation for
tenured faculty was so controversial that it could not be
discussed openly in most colleges and universities (Reisman,
1986). He compared it with the situation that occurs in psy-
chotherapy when patients ignore a central reality, one that
seems obvious and important, in their personal situation;
therapists refer to it as "the elephant in the room" (p. 73).
Although many universities had some form of performance
evaluation of faculty—annual reviews for salary increments,
students' evaluation of courses, periodic reviews for promotion, for example—only a small number of universities actually had a formal institutional policy. The Association of
American Colleges (AAC) and the American Association of
University Professors (AAUP), which sponsored the
Commission on Academic Tenure in 1971, recommended
corrections for the deficiencies in the tenure system
(Bennett and Chater, 1984); several recommendations were
related to evaluating tenured faculty members. Posttenure
review began to really emerge as an issue in the early 1980s.

In 1982, the National Commission on Higher Education Issues identified posttenure review as a major issue facing higher education and recommended that a system of peer review be developed on campuses to help ensure faculty members' competence and to strengthen institutional quality (Licata, 1986). At the urging of the American Council on Education, a Wingspread Conference on periodic evaluation of tenured faculty was held in 1983 in cooperation with the AAUP (Reisman, 1986). The conference invited both proponents and opponents (such as the AAUP) of posttenure review to voice their beliefs. Harold Shapiro, then president of the University of Michigan, pointed out faculty members' fundamental concerns about this issue, noting that tenure is an anchor so ingrained in faculty perceptions of their roles that the academic community would be diminished and even ruptured by posttenure review. In fact, he went so far as to say that it is suspect for a university administrator or trustee to even speculate informally about the subject. Although it appeared that the elephant in the room was still invisible to many attendees at the Wingspread Conference, Shapiro concluded that periodic evaluation of tenured faculty was good personnel policy and can play a nurturing role in faculty development (Reisman, 1986). The awarding of and continued existence of tenure is not really the central issue in the current debates about tenure. The real issues today are honest faculty evaluation, including posttenure review; adequate faculty development, including posttenure development; and termination when appropriate, linked to effective evaluation (Perley, 1995). This monograph includes examples of how posttenure review and faculty development can work together, yet not be formally connected, to improve faculty instruction, intellectual contributions, and service.

Professor Charles M. Larsen was actually the one who introduced a "different kind of posttenure review, a system better termed *development*" (Reisman, 1986, p. 76). Larsen believed that the focus of such a review would be on the positive goals of faculty support and improvement, not just on the negative procedures designed to weed out individuals who may not be living up to their responsibilities. The concept of using performance evaluation for developmental purposes rather than for decisions about promotion, salary, or termination is not a new concept in the education literature, and the idea of two types of evaluation is discussed in a series of articles appearing in the 1960s (Reisman, 1986, p. 77). A distinction can be made between *formative evaluation* designed to provide useful feedback to guide an ongoing activity designed for improvement and *summative evaluation* "aimed at answering a question in a final or terminal way" (Geis, 1977, p. 25). Similarly, two types of posttenure review have been termed "self-evaluation" (formative) and "formal evaluation" (summative) (Sullivan, 1977, pp. 130–148). An earlier ASHE-ERIC Higher Education Report offered an overview of the factors influencing posttenure review, stated the support and opposition, and gave then current examples at colleges and universities (Licata, 1986). The report concluded that faculty development programs should be linked to a posttenure evaluation system. In other words, the formative should be linked to the summative. This strategy, while logical at first reading, goes against established management theory stating that evaluation should be separate from development (Meyer, Kay, and French, 1965). Research has shown that it is unrealistic to expect a single performance appraisal program to take care of all employee and institutional needs. A linked strategy would force the evaluator into a self-conflicting role as a counselor (trying to help improve faculty performance) while at the same time presiding as judge over the action to be taken on the same professor's salary. Separating the two functions could also avoid the potential problem with some faculty who may set their professional development goals too low if they know serious consequences would result from not achieving them.

A later work also discusses the need for posttenure review and expands the definition to include five different methods:

1. *Annual reviews*—A short-term performance assessment that is common at many institutions and is often linked to merit pay. In some settings, these reviews are perfunctory and not effective at providing feedback for long-term career development and overall performance.
2. *Summative (periodic/consequential)*—A comprehensive review of all tenured faculty conducted periodically. Improved plans are used and the results are assessed with consequences for nonperformance.

3. *Summative (triggered/consequential)*—The comprehensive review of selected tenured faculty that is usually triggered by unsatisfactory performance.
4. *Formative (departmental)*—A review centering on the establishment of a professional development plan emphasizing the institution's needs and individual faculty members' career interests. Developed with the department head or dean.
5. *Formative (individual)*—Periodic review of all tenured faculty focusing on specific performance areas and long-term career goals. This option does not question competence and does not include formal personnel action (Licata and Morreale, 1997).

According to Licata and Morreale, the most useful system of posttenure review is a combination of Option 2 (summative—periodic/consequential) and Option 4 (formative—departmental) (p. 36). Other research has shown that performance evaluation of tenured faculty is perceived (by a survey of department chairs and administrators) to be more effective than reports completed by faculty or departmental reviews, and that developmental reviews are perceived to be more effective than those tied to salary reviews (Reisman, 1986). In addition, faculty performance in scholarship or research is believed to be more easily influenced by development strategies than the teaching or service components of faculty performance, probably because research by its nature can be more easily quantified than the more ambiguous quality assessment of postsecondary teaching and service to the community. Critics of posttenure evaluation and development must understand that it is the *performance* (usually research, teaching, and service) of the tenured individual under evaluation (or development), not the tenure of the individual (Bennett and Chater, 1984). Although tenure itself is indeed under attack in many ways, it is more often a change or addition to tenure—such as adding posttenure review procedures—that is occurring today. One recent survey of 680 colleges and universities found that 61% of respondents had a posttenure review policy in place and that another 9% had such a policy under development (Harris, 1996).

These numbers are not surprising, given the increase in the public's calls for accountability and the decrease in

Although tenure itself is indeed under attack, it is more often a change or addition to tenure that is occurring today.

budgets at many state colleges and universities (Goodman, 1994). In addition, the federally mandated uncapping of the retirement age for college and university faculty that went into effect January 1, 1994, has added to the reasons that posttenure review is becoming more common. Many faculty are understandably worried, for "tenure does not provide an absolute right to continued employment. The periodic review of faculty performance is one manner of addressing the ever present need to ensure excellence in the university" (Olswang and Fantel, 1980, p. 30). Moreover, periodic reviews would not violate academic freedom, despite the pleas of many faculty to keep tenure as it is (Olswang and Fantel, 1980). Nevertheless, a faculty member at Colorado College points out that a system of formal posttenure review would cause the faculty to become angry (Cramer, 1997), believing that tenure review is a very high stress time for individuals and that academic departments like to think that they hire well, evaluate well early on, and award tenure to people who will function well to the end of their careers (see also Brittain, 1992).

The AAUP is moving toward a more positive opinion of posttenure review, with faculty development as the primary goal. The association's current policy, adopted in 1983, states that periodic formal evaluation of tenured faculty would bring little benefit and would incur unacceptable costs in money and time, and reduce creativity and collegial relationships (American Association of University Professors, 1997). The association also believes it could threaten academic freedom. A more recent report on the subject, however, issued by the AAUP's Committee on Academic Freedom and Tenure, admits that posttenure review is rapidly becoming a reality and that the association might as well create a set of guidelines for the establishment of a system for the periodic evaluation of tenured faculty (American Association of University Professors, 1997). The report states that if such a system is designed and implemented by the faculty in a form that properly protects academic freedom and tenure, it could offer a way of evaluating tenured faculty that supports professional development as well as professional responsibility. Subsection IV.B. of "Standards for Good Practice in Post-Tenure Review" suggests that posttenure review should be developmental and supported by institutional resources for professional development or a change in career direction (p. 11). The AAUP also suggests that if a formal development plan is used instead of posttenure review, the faculty and the institution should mutually create the plan. The AAUP seems to support the separation of evaluation and development. It makes sense that a formal system of posttenure review that has strong consequences for nonperformance not be tied to a professional development plan. Thus, faculty could plan high achievement goals with less fear of repercussion if they do not achieve those high goals.

As for faculty that are tenured, the continuous review through a formal evaluation and faculty development planning systems could be a constructive way to maintain the vitality of senior professors in a rapidly changing environment (Rice, 1996). It should be a time for feedback and acknowledgment from colleagues, supervisors, and others in a profession that is usually very private. Once a faculty member has achieved tenure and been promoted, fewer regular opportunities may occur for self-analysis. These processes of reviewing senior faculty have "the potential for supporting resilient careers and the adaptability of faculty for what should be the capstone of their professional lives" (p. 31). Senior professors are not the only faculty who may need posttenure review and development, however. Relatively younger tenured faculty occasionally may not be interested in research, intellectual contributions, and, in general, changing their professional environment to help improve their performance and the institution—which may be one of the reasons that posttenure review policies are becoming more popular today in different types of institutions (Magner, 1996). Some of the impetus has come from state legislators, boards of trustees, and colleges and universities themselves. A common theme in many of the articles, reports, and statements about posttenure review is the importance, when assessing practices of evaluation, of determining a program's outcomes and effectiveness in promoting faculty development and productivity (Licata and Morreale, 1997; Neal, 1988). Clearly, a need exists to look further at the development of responsible and effective faculty evaluation and development systems that consider enhancing the growth of the faculty member (Rifkin, 1995).

The Need for Posttenure Faculty Development

It is up to both administrators and faculty to work together to carry out these important evaluative and developmental tasks. In most institutions today, faculty vary in their level of vitality. They "can be categorized into one of three types: self-directed faculty who renew themselves and can be productive with little external encouragement; minimalist faculty who produce little no matter what the incentives; and a large group of ambivalent faculty who could go either way" (Nelson, 1981, cited in Parker, 1991, p. 656). As faculty, administrators, and/or students in colleges and universities, we all know of some faculty who are high performers and some who are the "dying embers or lumps of charcoal—the dreaded deadwood of academe" (p. 656). These deadwood faculty and the larger group of ambivalent professors are the individuals who can and need to be continually renewed and developed, because faculty are the essence of the educational institution. A study conducted in 1976 diagrams students' ratings of a sample of almost 9,000 faculty from approximately 100 colleges in the United States on a 5-point Likert scale of perceived teaching effectiveness (Centra, 1976). Nontenured faculty in their first or second year of teaching received the lowest ratings, while both tenured and nontenured faculty with 3 to 12 years of experience received the highest ratings. Ratings dropped for tenured faculty with more than 12 years of experience (see Figure 1).

FIGURE 1

Ratings of Teacher Effectiveness by Years of Teaching

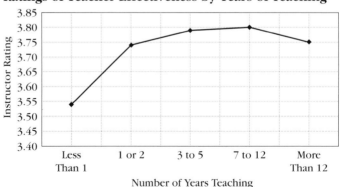

Source: Centra, 1985, p. 152. Reprinted with permission of the publisher.

These results seem to suggest that development strategies for posttenure faculty should focus extra attention on senior tenured professors with more than 12 years of experience. An analysis of student evaluations for all 37 full-time faculty (31 tenured) in a professional school at a midsized private college in fall 1998 (Alstete, 1999) found a similar increase, plateau, and slight decrease in ratings for faculty with more than 12 years of teaching experience. These results may be influenced by institutional policies and the organizational culture that encourage faculty to embrace primarily scholarly study in disciplinary areas. For a long time, administrations supported this concept: College teaching tends to be a profession in which knowledge of subject matter is the top priority and teaching is given secondary attention, while public school elementary and secondary teachers have been giving primary concern to teaching and secondary attention to subject matter (Eble and McKeachie, 1990). This situation may change as postsecondary education continues to evolve in the efficient, competitive marketplace of the 21st century.

At the current time, however, intellectual contributions in the form of recognized peer-reviewed research is still important to many institutions and accrediting agencies. A research study in fall 1992 found that tenured postsecondary faculty produced on average more articles or creative works, books or monographs, or other works during the previous 2 years than nontenured postsecondary faculty (see Table 1). While tenured faculty did produce more research, the results also show that the rate of output for articles/creative works for tenured faculty decreased from 3.6 to 3.3 per faculty member from 1987 to 1992. The number and quality of refereed journal articles is still a widely used benchmark for estimating the quality of faculty, which may be the result of the perceived importance of intellectual activity to stay current in academic disciplines and the easily quantifiable nature of measuring this output. Therefore, tenured faculty should be encouraged and motivated to continue producing research articles while at the same time developing their teaching skills.

The number of senior tenured faculty members continues to increase. As stated, senior faculty are now the largest cohort of faculty in colleges and universities (Finkelstein, 1993; Finkelstein and Jemmott, 1993). But what do these

TABLE 1

Average Research Production of Full-Time Postsecondary Faculty During the Previous Two Years

Tenure status, academic rank, and control of institution	Fall 1987				Fall 1992			
	Articles/ creative works	Books/ monographs	Presentations/ exhibits	Other	Articles/ creative works	Books/ monographs	Presentations/ exhibits	Other
Total	3.2	0.6	4.3	1.7	2.9	0.6	4.4	1.4
Tenure status								
Tenured	3.6	0.7	4.3	2.0	3.3	0.7	4.6	1.7
Not tenured	2.7	0.5	4.3	1.3	2.3	0.4	4.1	1.1
Academic rank								
Full professor	4.3	0.9	4.6	2.4	4.2	0.9	5.3	1.9
Associate professor	3.8	0.8	4.7	1.8	3.0	0.7	4.9	1.5
Assistant professor	2.9	0.5	4.8	1.4	2.8	0.5	4.4	1.3
Instructor/lecturer	1.2	0.2	2.8	1.1	0.9	0.2	2.2	0.6
Other/not applicable	1.2	0.1	3.4	0.7	1.2	0.2	3.4	1.0
Control of institution								
Public	3.2	0.6	4.4	1.8	2.9	0.6	4.4	1.4
Private	3.2	0.7	4.3	1.4	2.9	0.7	4.4	1.4

Source: National Center, 1988, 1993.

faculty care about, and what are their concerns? A recent study explored the experiences of midcareer and older faculty members in higher education through a qualitative study of 20 associate professors (15 men and 5 women) between the ages of 41 and 59 at a Canadian university (Karpiak, 1997). Nondirective interviews of these "graying" professors included discussions about their satisfaction and struggles in relation to their students, their own academic work with the university, and the administration. Figure 2 shows the results, identifying four attitudes characteristic of this group of mostly tenured professors: Meaning, Malaise, Marginality, and Mattering.

The schema represented in Figure 2 maps out the four central quadrants and the concepts and attitudes that emerged from the study. *Meaning,* in the upper right quadrant, refers to faculty members' high interest and caring with regard to academic responsibilities. *Malaise,* in the upper left quadrant, represents faculty members' low interest and caring, which may include loss of meaning, stagnation, and a sense of triviality and unimportance in what they are doing. Malaise is also closely related to burnout—emotional exhaustion, depersonalization, and reduced personal accomplishments (Farber, 1983, cited in Karpiak, 1997, p. 30). *Marginality,* in the lower left quadrant, represents faculty members' view of the university as a place of low interest and caring. It also refers to the degree to which individuals feel distanced from the institution, outside the mainstream of their sphere—the university, colleagues, students, or even their own discipline (Karpiak, 1997). *Mattering,* in the lower right quadrant, represents faculty members' view of the institution as high in interest and caring.

This study illuminates several features that may be useful to administrators and faculty developers concerned with the predicament that college and university faculty face at midcareer (tenure) and midlife: the dynamic nature of the relationship between tenured faculty and the institution; the importance individual perceptions can have in shaping individuals' behavior; the mutual interaction among the four quadrants in the schema; and the ability of faculty to move among some or all of the quadrants over their career.

Another related study investigated academic policy development at 80 research universities with regard to the academic labor market, academic reward structure, faculty

FIGURE 2

A Schema of Faculty and University Interest and Caring

Faculty Member

MALAISE
Expression: "I'm not as good as I could be; I'm not as good as I was."
Features: Burnout, trivial pursuit, need for renewal, thinking of retirement.

Evidence in Research: Low interest in research: Some peaked early; efforts to publish are frustrated; Still hoping for "the gold."
Evidence in Teaching: Teaching is stressful, unrewarding; low self-esteem, self-blame, puzzled; blame students' low quality and motivation; see students "on the road to nowhere"; alienation, depersonalization; distressed over age gap with students; hope/desire for renewal—a surge.

MEANING
Expression: ". . . I'd probably come back and teach seminars."

Features: Define what or whom they care about; satisfaction with the academic work; concern extended to others.
Evidence in Research: High among women and younger men; moderate interest, yet ongoing for older.
Evidence in Teaching: High interest in teaching; seen as a vocation; mentoring, guiding, watching; see students full of hope, "a good crop"; despair over distance from students; try new teaching approaches; seek out new direction, new areas of study; find strength in areas of competence; find meaning regardless of not mattering.

Low Interest and Caring

High Interest and Caring

MARGINALITY
EXPRESSION: "I'm a ghost."

Features: Feeling "out of things," on the periphery; not part of the big picture.

Evidence: Low collegiality, isolated, excluded; low investment in the university; angry, stubborn, frustrated; women feel unaccepted, unentitled; exacerbated by disruption in career or loss of grant funds; teaching and service are seen as devalued; new theories in field render them "a maker of buggy whips"; made worse if in a small subdiscipline or area of study; made worse when research is highly specialized; may turn to family and/or external pursuits; waiting to ride that wave again.

MATTERING
EXPRESSION: "The market has turned against people of our generation."
Features: Administration is interested in us and depends on us; administration is concerned with our fate.
Evidence: The absence of evidence in this quadrant is a primary feature of this study. Instead, faculty feel left out of problem solving and decision making; feel unappreciated, unacknowledged; "The human element is mission."; administrators are "ghostly figures," not visible; less of a concern for younger faculty; in crises, visits from administrators are appreciated; the value of a "thank you" for work done.

The University

Source: Karpiak, 1997. Used with permission.

seniority and retirement, and institutional research and planning (Crawley, 1995). The results confirmed the need for more flexible academic personnel policies in support of tenured faculty development. Tenured faculty need to have support and opportunities for development that are flexible enough to address the various states and attitudes faculty may be in today. Whatever organizational structures institutions develop, they must satisfy both the college and individual needs.

Summary

This first section has explored who tenured faculty members are today, how their age and rank place in the overall population of faculty in higher education, and what some challenges facing them are today, such as new technology, new students, academic freedom, and posttenure review. Tenured faculty members are not going away, and institutions of higher education must address these faculty members' needs and the institutions' needs for outcomes assessment and continuous improvement. The 21st century will undoubtedly see a continued influx and use of information and instructional technology that will likely change the way new, incoming students expect to be served by their college and university faculty. "Knowledge management," "outcomes assessment," "active learning," "collaborative learning," "service learning"—these are just some of the phrases that are changing the landscape of higher education and adding to the chorus of concern about tenure and tenured faculty. Clearly, faculty development must be explored further and ways examined to build a system of improvement and appreciation using policies and programs that serve tenured faculty.

HOW HAS HIGHER EDUCATION RESPONDED TO THIS CONCERN?

What has been and can be done to help develop faculty as professionals, become more productive, improve their teaching, and become more satisfied with their work? This section discusses some of the literature on psychological and organizational development that has influenced theory and practice in higher education. It then explores the history and roots of faculty development in colleges and universities, defines faculty development with examples of current models, and, finally, examines the link between faculty development and posttenure review.

Managing and developing employees properly, especially highly educated and experienced professionals who have a tenure contract, is a complex undertaking. Much of the literature on professional development states that the development of an individual is a series of steps involving the knowledge, skills, and values that educators need to realize their full potential (Kydd, Crawford, and Riches, 1997). Professional development has much to do with the realization of one's potential, a process that is built upon the acquisition of knowledge, skills, and relevant theoretical perspectives. To help faculty achieve their full potential, administrators and others should work toward creating organizational cultures that recognize that people are different and have different professional aspirations. The principles that are taught in psychology and business management courses, such as Maslow's hierarchy of needs (Maslow, 1970) and the application of these theories (Rogers, 1967), are worth revisiting to help understand the creation of proper conditions for the full development of tenured faculty. McGregor's concept of contrasting the positive and negative beliefs about employees (Theory X and Theory Y assumptions) makes it easier to see that management of faculty can be enhanced by understanding that not all tenured individuals are incapable of further development (McGregor, 1960). This report examines primarily programs for those faculty who can develop (Theory X), and explains some alternatives for Theory Y faculty. The fundamental idea is that people are different and that they learn and grow in different ways. Some interesting alternative definitions of intelligence have been emerging in recent years—logical, spatial, practical (Handy, 1990), emotional, intuitive, and intellectual

(Postle, 1989). Motivating these different types of intelligence can be a challenge, and attention to motivational factors is an important starting point for the selection of effective management styles (Kydd and others, 1997).

People tend to work harder when the culture of the organization satisfies their motivational needs of feeling supported, heard, noticed, encouraged, trusted, informed, and challenged. Employees are highly motivated when they find the work itself intrinsically satisfying and challenging, feel they have a role in decision making, and are involved in the management of the organization (Herzberg, 1966). Further, employees are poorly motivated when there are too many rules and regulations governing personal and professional activity. A major goal of development programs should be to help faculty realize their full potential through processes and mechanisms that release and empower, not excessively control and supervise. Posttenure faculty development should involve strategies, perhaps through programs created by and for tenured faculty, that establish a shared vision by all that these policies of faculty development foster both personal and organizational development.

Developmental psychology offers some useful ideas to help understand how a professional development program can help different types of faculty by understanding that they may be at different points in their career and life. Just as most humans pass through a number of phases and stages throughout their life (Erikson, 1977), most faculty can also be seen to develop in a career cycle:

1. *Launching the career;*
2. *Stabilizing: developing mature commitment[,] feeling at ease, seeking more responsibility;*
3. *[Facing] new challenges and concerns, diversifying, seeking added responsibilities;*
4. *Reaching a professional plateau: reappraisal, sense of mortality, ceasing striving for promotion or stagnating and becoming cynical; [and]*
5. *Preparing for retirement: focusing disenchantment, serenity (Leithwood, 1990, cited in Kydd and others, 1997, p. 24).*

For tenured faculty, development might focus on stages three through five.

The concept of career stages may not often be discussed at planning meetings for development activities because of their sensitive nature. Perhaps they should be discussed, however, because career stages can often be a problem when examining faculty careers (Clark and Corcoran, 1989). Tenured faculty may require new challenges to keep them interested—team teaching, joint research projects, or learning to use new technology—and/or new responsibilities—being a mentor to a more junior professor, for example. Tenured faculty members usually have more experience than nontenured faculty—an important point because psychologists have learned that practical knowledge, such as teaching and research skills, is acquired or learned from experience (Jarvis, 1997). Midcareer is often an unproductive and unrewarding phase as individuals wonder whether this is all there is to their careers and their lives in general. Moreover, both midcareer and senior faculty groups at some institutions in one survey felt threatened by the new emphasis on research, relegated to subordinate status, resentful toward an ungrateful administration, and suspicious of better-trained junior colleagues (Bowen and Schuster, 1986, pp. 149–150). Posttenure faculty development should concentrate on reducing midcareer and senior faculty members' negative feelings associated with career stages, and help them to use their vast experience for the benefit of the students, the institution, and themselves.

Tenured faculty may require new challenges to keep them interested.

Modern developmental psychologists have rethought the concept of career staging, which no longer adheres to the strict age and stage concepts of one's life span (Knefelkamp, 1990). Adult and academic career life can be viewed as a fluid cycle of seasons, where individuals revisit tasks, challenges, phases, and stages dozens of times during an academic career. The seasons of an academic career can include several "discoveries":

1. Discovering the power of words, ideas, and conversations;
2. Discovery of the faculty role;
3. Discovery of the student;
4. Discovery of public self beyond the classroom in areas such as research, teaching, and administration;
5. Discovery of multiple competing commitments for professional and personal roles;

6. Discovery of the need to stop teaching;
7. Discovery of feeling marginal or left out; and
8. Discovery of the courage to be creative despite fear and doubt.

Faculty development leaders need to plan strategies to see the larger picture and support faculty as individuals while working to create and maintain the balance and harmony of the academic community (Atkins, Hagseth, and Arnold, 1990). As faculty move between and among their seasons of discovery in the academic community, it is important to encourage and reward continued learning and development.

Management and organizational theorists have also written about learning organizations and organizational learning. Organizational learning is the process of "detection and correction of errors" (Argyris and Schön, 1978). In this view, organizations learn through individuals acting as agents for them: "The individuals' learning activities, in turn, are facilitated or inhibited by an ecological system of factors that may be called an organizational learning system" (p. 117). Four constructs related to information systems are integrally linked to organizational learning: knowledge acquisition, information distribution, information interpretation, and organizational memory (Huber, 1991). Learning need not be conscious or intentional, and it need not result in observable changes in behavior (Huber, 1991). From Huber's behavioral perspective, learning occurs if, through the processing of information, the range of potential behaviors is changed. This idea that potential behaviors can be changed in an organization because of the way that information is acquired, processed, and distributed may be quite appropriate for faculty in higher education today. It can be important given the incredible growth of instructional technology, distance learning, new approaches to teaching such as active learning, and the demands by employers that college graduates be able to critically analyze and communicate information.

Learning organizations (which, one hopes, institutions of higher education consider themselves) are defined as organizations in which an individual cannot *not* learn, because learning is insinuated into the fabric of life in the organization (Senge, 1990). Moreover, a learning organization is a group of people continually enhancing their capacity to create what they want to create (Senge, 1990). Such organizations have an ingrained philosophy for anticipating, reacting to, and responding to change, complexity, and uncertainty. The concept of a learning organization is increasingly relevant, given the increasing complexity and uncertainty of the organizational environment (and higher education). The rate at which organizations learn may become the only sustainable source of competitive advantage (Senge, 1990). But how have colleges and universities traditionally encouraged faculty learning in their organizations?

The History and Roots of Faculty Development

Colleges historically have expected faculty members to be responsible for their own personal and professional development (Centra, 1985). Because most early colleges and universities were religious institutions, the majority of faculty members before the Civil War were clergymen (Rudolph, 1977). Faculty development for those instructors primarily consisted of maintaining spiritual and moral resolve. As institutions' missions and the quantity of ideas within them broadened, faculty found themselves responsible for keeping up to date in their fields of knowledge. The sabbatical leave was begun at Harvard in 1810 (Blackburn, Pellino, Boberg, and O'Connell, 1980). Some other, more affluent universities added paid leaves of absence and sabbaticals in the late 19th century. Before the 1960s, colleges and universities did not have well defined and comprehensive faculty development programs; the main practices involved orientation for new faculty, sabbaticals, and support to attend conferences (Centra, 1985). A small number of institutions did have instructional improvement programs in the late 1960s, including Syracuse University, Michigan State University, McGill University, and the University of Minnesota. Their programs primarily concentrated on assisting faculty volunteers to analyze and solve instructional problems. This *instructional development* model was one of three components of faculty development that emerged in the 1970s (Centra, 1985), with *personal development* and *organizational development* also identified as related components (Bergquist and Phillips, 1975). A related study of 55 colleges and universities added *curriculum development* as well (Gaff, 1975).

In the mid-1970s, faculty development appeared to be gaining popularity at colleges and universities in the United

LIBRARY
UNIVERSITY OF ST. FRANCIS
JOLIET, ILLINOIS

States. A major study of institutions in the United States in 1976 found that approximately 60% reported a set of faculty development practices and that another 3% were planning such programs (Centra, 1985, p. 146). Four groups of development practices seemed to define faculty development practices in that study: high faculty involvement, instructional assistance practices, traditional practices, and emphasis on assessment. On many of the campuses surveyed, the faculty most needing improvement (newer faculty and those at the end of their careers—see Table 2) were minimally involved.

This finding is understandable, as participation in most development activities was voluntary; moreover, newer faculty probably take some time to learn what programs are available at the institution, and more experienced tenured faculty probably feel they have learned all they can. In general, the faculty may also sense the institution's ambiguous efforts toward their personal and professional growth, and, as noted, higher education has traditionally emphasized primarily scholarly study (Boyer, 1990).

The 1970s and early 1980s have been called the era of definition and wide dispersion of information on faculty

TABLE 2

Estimates of Faculty Involvement in Development Activities

	Percentage of 756 institutional respondents				
	Very few	*Some*	*About half*	*Most*	*No response*
Younger faculty in their first years of teaching	13	31	23	27	06
Faculty with over 15 or 20 years of teaching experience	22	45	17	09	07
Non-tenured faculty	08	34	25	19	14
Tenured faculty	09	41	23	10	17
Good teachers who want to get better	03	21	28	43	05
Faculty who really need to improve	40	38	08	06	08

Source: Centra, 1985, p. 151. Reprinted with permission of the publisher.

development in higher education (Finkelstein, 1990). The Fund for the Improvement of Postsecondary Education (FIPSE) and several private foundations, including the Danforth, W. K. Kellogg, Mellon, Carnegie, and Ford Foundations, have provided external support and helped fund faculty development. The Bush Foundation Faculty Development Project in Minnesota, begun in 1980 to study faculty development closely at a variety of institutions (Eble and McKeachie, 1985), funded faculty development programs in three states that also served faculty from around the country. Its aim was to improve undergraduate education through individually developed programs that were funded initially for 3 years at 30 institutions. Analysis and evaluation of these programs showed that successful faculty development programs were faculty driven (with administrative support), used local expertise, and had follow-up activities. It also found that faculty members' ideas about their individual development were not necessarily reliable guides to what might best serve student learning (Eble and McKeachie, 1985, pp. 35–36).

Another sign that faculty development was becoming more institutionalized in the 1970s was the formation, in 1976, of the Professional and Organizational Development (POD) Network in Higher Education (Koerin, 1980). The title of this organization reflects the connection between the institution's human resources (the faculty) and the organization itself. The group comprises a network of professionals involved in faculty and organizational development who share a commitment to improving higher education through a professional association. At this writing, the POD Network is still active, holding annual conferences and workshops, publishing materials, and maintaining a Web site. (Appendix A contains more information about the POD Network and other resources on faculty development.)

Evaluation of faculty, including tenured faculty, became a popular concept (a buzzword) in the 1980s, with institutions wanting to increase their yield with a limited supply of faculty, respond to criticisms from outside agencies, and prepare for the impending elimination of the mandatory retirement age (Clark, Corcoran, and Lewis, 1990). A comprehensive review of the literature for 1965 to 1985 found that the references to faculty development could be categorized into 49 strategies in 3 areas: institution; department/college;

and individual faculty or administrators (Bland and Schmitz, 1988, pp. 193–195. The most frequently mentioned strategies were workshops, sabbaticals and leaves, evaluation of faculty, and growth or professional development plans. The use of professional development plans has also turned out to be a key element of successful posttenure faculty development programs. The researchers also found that most of the literature was written in the last few years of the study, suggesting that the topic was growing in interest. Some recommendations are mentioned frequently:

- Faculty development should be linked to the institution's mission and policies;
- The programs should be an integral, ongoing, visible, and important part of the institution;
- Programs should be directly and properly supported by the administration.

A similar search of the literature for 1989 to 1997 (using Dissertation Abstracts International [DAI], Sociology, PsychInfo, Medline, and, most important, ERIC) showed an initial increase in the early 1990s and a slight upward trend in recent years for the amount of literature on faculty development (see Figure 3). Interest in faculty development has grown, and many leading researchers, writers, and practitioners in education continue to view it as a significant topic. Although a significant amount of descriptive literature exists on how individual colleges and universities have engaged in effective and varied faculty development programs, there is no clearly defined supporting theory underlying faculty development (Aleamoni, 1990). Likewise, no underlying theory exists for posttenure faculty development.

Faculty development is related to faculty evaluation (Smith, 1976). Many of the recent books and articles on faculty evaluation strategies have provided and/or disseminated widely accepted and used evaluation strategies with specific measures of effectiveness (Braskamp and Ory, 1994; Licata, 1986). But for faculty development strategies, the related challenge is to find representative and accurate outcome measures (Aleamoni, 1990). Assessment of outcomes is important for continuous improvement of the processes. Programs today, the expertise of the faculty development staff, the location of the office in the organizational

FIGURE 3

Results of Literature Search for "Faculty Development"

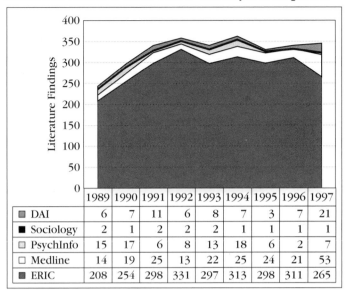

	1989	1990	1991	1992	1993	1994	1995	1996	1997
▦ DAI	6	7	11	6	8	7	3	7	21
■ Sociology	2	1	2	2	2	1	1	1	1
☐ PsychInfo	15	17	6	8	13	18	6	2	7
☐ Medline	14	19	25	13	22	25	24	21	53
▦ ERIC	208	254	298	331	297	313	298	311	265

hierarchy, the funding, and the intended audience vary widely. As mentioned earlier, directly linking development and evaluation strategies may not always be the best approach.

A survey of all U.S. colleges and universities in 1975 estimated that half of the institutions offered some form of faculty development activities and reported that 40% claimed to have separate faculty development units on their campuses (Centra, 1976). Further, the study supported the wide variety of programs and reported which of them faculty development directors judged most effective. A factor analysis that resulted in six factors or groups of practices that were most common included instructional assistance practices, an emphasis on assessment, and traditional practices. Overall, faculty development activities in the 1970s challenged traditional efforts to keep faculty up to date in their disciplines through sabbaticals, travel to professional meetings, development grants, and other such support. Some writers argued that different activities were needed (Bergquist and Phillips, 1977; Group for Human Development in Higher Education,

1974; Erickson, 1986; Freedman, 1973; Gaff, 1975; Smith, 1976), such as stronger support for teaching. The POD Network conducted a survey of faculty development practices in 1975 and found that 40% of the 4-year institutions surveyed had at least one person responsible for faculty development. In the late 1970s and early 1980s, several more systematic efforts attempted to evaluate faculty development programs (Blackburn and others, 1980; Eble and McKeachie, 1985; Erickson, 1986; Erickson and Erickson, 1979; Hoyt and Howard, 1978; Nelson and Siegel, 1980). These studies varied in their approaches and methodologies, and reached different conclusions. Some emphasized the increasing importance of developing faculty members' understanding of newer, nontraditional undergraduate students and their different learning styles; factors influencing the success of faculty development programs, such as ownership, administrative support, and outside consultants; and the importance of faculty members' desire to improve in the program's success.

The two major studies cited (Erickson, 1986; Centra, 1978) surveyed colleges and universities across the United States in an attempt to estimate the extent of faculty development activity (Sell and Chism, 1991). Centra's study contacted 2,600 presidents of universities and 4-year and 2-year colleges, while Erickson contacted 1,600 chief academic officers of universities and 4-year colleges. Although the selected populations differed and the studies were conducted 10 years apart, the questions followed a similar line of questioning. When the two studies are looked at together, they provide a general overview of faculty development activity. The later POD study (Erickson, 1986) found that 63% of the colleges and universities surveyed had an organized system for the development and improvement of instruction. In contrast, the earlier Centra study found only 40% with an organized system. The POD survey also found that resources for assessing and improving teaching were widely available (97%) through students' ratings of instruction and other activities. Also available on nearly all campuses were professional development grants, leaves, or exchanges (96%), and workshops or seminars (88%) (Erickson, 1986). In addition, for tenured faculty, at least one-fourth of the institutions responding did offer services that engage midcareer faculty in coping with stress, increasing writing productivity, and managing time effectively.

The increasing awareness of faculty development in higher education has been assisted by the Teachers Insurance and Annuity Association/College Retirement Equities Fund (TIAA-CREF), the nation's largest retirement system in education. TIAA-CREF sponsors the annual Theodore M. Hesburgh Award, which presents $30,000 to the winner and highlights the importance of teaching and learning at colleges and universities, a major component of faculty development programs. The Hesburgh Award helps point out that varying definitions and aspects of faculty development exist at different institutions. It acknowledges and rewards successful, innovative faculty development programs that enhance undergraduate teaching and help inspire the growth of such initiatives at this country's colleges and universities. The faculty development programs under consideration each year are judged to see which best meet the three award criteria: significance of the program in higher education, appropriate program rationale, and successful results and impact on undergraduate teaching and students' learning. The 1998 winner was Brooklyn College, City University of New York, for its multifaceted faculty development program called Transformations. The plan builds awareness of the critical importance of integrating first-year students into the college community. Its nontraditional design requires faculty members to establish connections between courses and consider what analytic skills and disciplinary perspectives should be represented across the curriculum. To date, 110 tenured faculty have taught in the block programs for freshman students. Certificate of excellence recipients in 1997 included the Faculty Development Institute at Virginia Polytechnic Institute and State University (Virginia Tech). At Virginia Tech, the institution has reinforced its commitment to quality education by emphasizing that undergraduate courses will be taught by full-time faculty, including its most distinguished members (tenured faculty).

Overall, the history and literature on faculty development show an evolving pattern of activities that are becoming more widely used at colleges and universities. Personal, instructional, curriculum, and organizational development strategies have been developing in a variety of ways at many institutions. But how, specifically, is faculty development defined, particularly for tenured faculty?

What Does Faculty Development Mean?

Several definitions of faculty development have been found in the literature. One such definition describes faculty development as "an institutional process [that] seeks to modify the attitudes, skill, and behavior of faculty members toward greater competence and effectiveness in meeting student needs, their own needs and the needs of the institution" (Francis, 1975, p. 720, cited in Stordahl, 1981, p. 9). Faculty development is a widely used phrase that has both a broad and a narrow definition. Broadly, it covers a wide range of activities that have as their overall goal the improvement of students' learning, some through long-range processes. More narrowly, the phrase is aimed at helping faculty members improve their competence as teachers and scholars (Eble and McKeachie, 1985). Faculty development programs vary in their purpose, but they are commonly designed to enhance personal and professional development, instructional development, and/or organizational development. Professional development involves promoting faculty growth and enabling faculty members to obtain and enhance job-related skills, knowledge, and awareness. Instructional development involves the preparation of learning materials, styles of instruction, and the updating of courses. Organizational development focuses on creating an effective institutional atmosphere in which faculty and faculty development personnel can implement new practices for teaching and learning (Gaff, 1975). Personal development involves a more holistic approach to help faculty members enhance interpersonal skills, promote wellness, and assist with career planning (Graf, Albright, and Wheeler, 1992). Curriculum development overlaps with professional, instructional, organizational, and personal development, and involves the development of additional scholarly and teaching competencies, the creation of new instructional materials, and the development of new communication and organizational patterns (Bergquist and Phillips, 1975; Eble and McKeachie, 1985). On the basis of these interpretations, posttenure faculty development can be defined as those activities that seek to improve students' learning, scholarship, and service in higher education by developing personal, instructional, organizational, and curricular aspects of faculty members who have earned tenure.

While faculty development centers at colleges and universities are usually geared toward all faculty members, both tenured and nontenured, some of the activities can be of special benefit to the more experienced and tenured professionals. Centers often offer one-on-one consultations with individual faculty and group activities such as seminars, workshops, peer support group meetings, newsletters, mentoring programs, orientation for new faculty, travel grant programs, and resource libraries (Graf and others, 1992). Tenured faculty, with significant teaching experience as a basis upon which to reflect and more effectively learn, often find instructional development activities rewarding. These activities may involve either the methods used in the learning environment or the actual learning materials employed in the learning environment. Common topics include basic course design or revision, preparation of learning activities for students, and adoption or development of learning materials such as books, videos, and computer software. Often these topics are discussed by experienced faculty in a group setting, where instructional skills and the general outlook toward teaching can be greatly enhanced.

Those faculty development programs that touch on organizational development can also greatly benefit tenured faculty. Such organization-related activities may involve training in management and interpersonal relations for department chairs (often tenured faculty), discussion of issues related to instructional facilities and technology, and assistance for the institution and individual departments in setting goals and in strategic planning. Some specialized and professional accrediting organizations require that the organization involve a broad base of faculty in such strategic and operational planning processes for the department and institution to receive professional accreditation (American Assembly, 1994). Therefore, organizational development involving tenured faculty can be a critically important activity for many schools and colleges. Personal development activities usually focus on strategies and experiences that look at and develop intra- and interpersonal effectiveness, which may include career planning programs, assertiveness development, and personal attending skills that are taught

Faculty development programs that touch on organizational development can greatly benefit tenured faculty.

through individual consultations, workshops and seminars, peer support group meetings, and off-campus retreats (Graf and others, 1992).

In 1979, the Association of American Colleges organized the Project on Faculty Development to evaluate faculty renewal programs at 20 colleges that had undertaken comprehensive faculty development programs during the previous 5 years (Nelson and Siegel, 1980). The authors grouped the findings into four areas related to the definitions stated earlier. Professional development referred to a faculty member's continuing growth as a scholar and contributor to the intellectual community on campus and in the discipline, while instructional development focused on programs designed to encourage faculty to share new and previously successful ideas about teaching (p. 7). Curriculum change (or development) and organizational change could also provide useful opportunities for faculty renewal. The authors of that study did not find many campuses in the AAC survey that conducted much organizational development with faculty. Teaching and research support seemed to be the more common strategies for most of the faculty development efforts uncovered.

This statement is supported by a study conducted in 1984 that analyzed the perceptions of administrative support for teaching and faculty development (McFerron and others, 1990). The survey collected information from 142 deans, 392 department chairs, and 1,173 faculty members about their beliefs regarding availability of funds for teaching support and faculty development, the importance of teaching in tenure decisions and merit salary adjustments, and the level of support for faculty attendance at professional meetings. Although deans reported a high importance placed on teaching quality, faculty tended to report lower importance for teaching and research and higher importance for publishing and committee work with regard to tenure, merit pay, and development support (pp. 1–3). The authors of the study make a strong point about the supposed double-talk of deans with regard to teaching versus research, but there is no great love of teaching support implied because one of the authors' main conclusions is faculty members' perceived lack of travel and sabbatical money. Others have noted that faculty, especially at research institutions, are rarely trained to teach as part of their graduate education and that teaching ability is usually not examined during interviews before hiring (Altman, 1986, p. 51). In addition, promotions, tenure, and termination tend to be based on research performance, and faculty at research institutions tend not to view themselves as employees of the institution but as contractual consultants to the university. These parameters, combined with a wide lack of meaningful departmental supervision, are some of the reasons that many faculty development programs tend to be incremental or patchwork, nonsequential, and short term (Altman, 1986). Faculty development programs should be specifically designed to the individualities of the institution, be designed by and for the faculty, and involve the department chairs in planning and running the programs.

Merit salary adjustments or policies regarding merit pay are finding their way into the salary structure of more and more colleges and universities each year as competition among institutions grows (Blum, 1989). Typically, a merit pay system allocates money to each academic department within the institution for merit raises based on the total pool of funds available for faculty salaries. Deans often keep a portion for awarding faculty at their own discretion, while most of the money is given to the department head, who then uses his or her own policy to make the individual awards. Often these award decisions are made upon the recommendation of faculty committees and require the approval of the dean, vice president for academic affairs, and/or the president. Merit pay for faculty was originally more common at large research universities, where the emphasis in faculty assessment is on the number of research publications. These institutions also have a broad range of faculty salaries because of the pressures of the academic job market for high-performing research faculty (Blum, 1989). A definite movement is also apparent by community colleges and other types of institutions to start recognizing the contributions of outstanding faculty members (including tenured professors) (Andrews, 1987). Merit pay can be an effective development tool for many tenured faculty.

Before posttenure faculty development is examined further, it is important to further explore the development models defined in the higher education literature. Doing so will help place strategies for tenured faculty into a broader understanding of general faculty development today.

Models of Faculty Development

A previous Higher Education Report, *Faculty Development and Evaluation in Higher Education* (Smith, 1976), examined several of the concepts, models, and definitions available at that time, including Gaff's widely cited model (Gaff, 1975). Gaff identifies three conceptions of improvement: faculty development (also called faculty renewal), instructional development, and organizational development. In this model, faculty development concentrates on faculty members to promote faculty growth and help faculty members acquire knowledge and skills related to teaching and learning. Instructional development focuses on courses and curricula, with goals that include improvement in students' learning and preparation of learning material by the faculty. Organizational development helps to create an effective environment for teaching and learning through improved interpersonal relationships, team building, and policies that generally support effective teaching and learning.

In 1975, Bergquist and Phillips offered a model that is similar to Gaff's, which was then later expanded to extend the ideas of both (Bergquist and Phillips, 1977). In that model, faculty development included personal development, instructional development, and organizational development. Gaff's idea of faculty development contains elements of what Bergquist and Phillips call personal and instructional development, while Gaff's concept of instructional development focuses more closely on course and curriculum design. An important difference between the two models is that Gaff believes that any of the three aspects (personal, instructional, and organizational development) can be implemented without reference to the other two. Bergquist and Phillips believe that instructional development is the logical start. They also believe that all three elements should be present in a mature faculty development program, with personal and organizational development secondary to instructional development. Bergquist and Phillips then added the concept of community development, which is a concern with the entire environment of an institution (1977). This third model indicates how activities in instructional development can have process-level outcomes but also affect the general organizational structure and attitude. In addition, the third model clarifies the focus of various kinds of efforts in this area by suggesting alternative approaches to development of the individual, the group, and the entire institution.

The discussion in the literature regarding types of faculty development continued in 1978 with a major work by John Centra. Centra stated that the Gaff and Bergquist/Phillips models are heuristic rather than empirical and set out to determine whether more appropriate ways can be found to categorize faculty development activities in institutions of higher education. He conducted a national study of 756 colleges and universities that grouped practices according to use: high faculty involvement, instructional assistance practices, traditional practices, and emphasis on assessment. These groups provide some evidence about the kinds of development programs actually employed at the time of the study. Centra found that larger institutions tended to hire full-time faculty development specialists who employ more traditional development efforts, such as sabbaticals and temporary reductions in teaching load, while smaller colleges were less able to afford specialists and used practices that were run by and for the faculty, such as the use of tenured teachers with expertise to help other faculty, including master teachers and teaching circles (committees). Centra's results provide a perspective of development programs somewhat different from the heuristic models offered by Gaff and Bergquist/Phillips. The instructional assistance category, however, does overlap with the earlier concept of instructional development.

The administration of the institution, often the chief academic officer or the dean's office in consultation with department chairs, can select which approach or combination of approaches should be supported. The decision should be based on the institution's needs and priorities and expected costs and benefits. A survey of 47 postsecondary districts in Texas found that although many institutions are actively trying to plan and conduct faculty development activities, greater assistance is needed (Lovelace and LaBrecque, 1991). In considering development of tenured faculty, the approaches chosen should consider how to best motivate tenured faculty and take advantage of their significant experience. In terms of the career life cycle of a typical professor, it would be natural to think that newer nontenured faculty need more instructional and personal development, while posttenure senior faculty can focus more on organizational development, because senior faculty with many years of experience may be able to look broadly at the institution's structure and the relationship among its units with regard to common activities such as workshops, seminars, and other support. Tenured faculty should be offered the option of helping the organization improve development activities and thereby help their fellow faculty develop. Several major outcomes are possible from organizational development:

- *Clarifying the relationship of development activities among units*
- *Diagnosing institutional problems*
- *Insuring communication and feedback*
- *Clarifying institutional or departmental goals*
- *Facilitating program implementation*
- *Improving institutional climate.* (Diamond, 1988, p. 10)

By believing that the administration and the institution respect all their years of experience and accumulated knowledge, tenured faculty can be motivated to help themselves and others develop their skills and knowledge. For example, faculty-created teaching committees or "circles" are a good way for senior faculty to take the lead in teaching improvement at an institution. The next section describes successful examples of teaching circles in which self-selected faculty garnered administrative support at public and private institutions to create a supportive climate that fosters professional growth through workshops and open dialogue among peer professionals.

These types of faculty teaching committees can be within one department or campus-wide activities. The one constant among these and other types of faculty development activities in different colleges and universities is in the variation among them (Wright, 1988). Structural variations among programs occur in how they are organized and where they are located within the institution, for example:

1. A single, campus-wide center *[that] is named, staffed and budgeted within the institution to accomplish targeted development goals. It serves the entire institution[,] or a substantial segment of it, in a variety of ways.*
2. A multi-campus, cooperative program *[that] coordinates programs and resources to serve several campuses in*

> **Tenured faculty should be offered the option of helping the organization improve development activities.**

meeting their faculty development needs in a variety of ways.

3. A special purpose center *[that] serves a specifically defined audience to accomplish more narrowly defined development goals.*
4. Development components *[that] are a part of a broader academic program. [They] often occur when resources or numbers to be served are relatively small.* (Wright, 1988, p. 14)

Tenured faculty are served by most of these structural types.

Each type has its strengths and weaknesses. Campus-wide centers are often the most comprehensive, with a full-time staff (usually a director and a support staff) and a budget for activities (often supported by grants). Programs at these kinds of centers are designed to serve a large audience and to stimulate change. They usually go beyond traditional grants, leaves, and travel, and offer skill-building workshops, seminars, conferences, retreats, and individual consultations. Multicampus cooperative programs usually have a central office that coordinates staff and administers resources for a number of institutions. Programs often include financial support for leaves, sabbaticals, fellowships, weekend and summer conferences, and discipline-based institutes. Of special interest to tenured faculty is the opportunity to interact with colleagues from other institutions and communicate with them through newsletters, special publications, and meetings. Special-purpose centers may be campus-wide or multicampus, and are designed with a specialized goal in mind rather than the broader objectives of the first two types. For example, centers may focus on career development, graduate teaching assistants, critical thinking, or course materials for freshman orientation. The development components of other academic programs offer similar activities and goals to campus-wide centers but are administered within a specific unit, such as a dean's office or a faculty development committee. Some professional schools within larger institutions, such as business or law schools, often have specialized centers that offer development tailored for their faculty. In addition, Centra (1978) found that 44% of all institutions had a unit or person responsible for development or instructional improvement, and some had decentralized units. Decentralization of some types of administrative structures in higher education has been correlated with increased effectiveness (Alstete, 1997).

As the literature on faculty development shows, different models exist for examining faculty development activities. Faculty development is the key issue in the broader area of professional development, which has been viewed as somewhat limited (Educational Resources Information Center, 1997). The five trends uncovered in this area are (a) faculty development, (b) professional development to instigate change in a profession or field, (c) mentoring, (d) professional standards for administrators, and (e) staff development (p. 1). A related model describes professional development activities (for faculty and staff) as a "deep-rooted, thick-trunked tree that lately has sprouted new branches" (Lindquist, 1981, p. 733). The base of this development tree is the training or education that individuals first receive as students themselves upon which research and scholarship are grown. The "new branches" include instructional development, personal development, networking, organizational development, higher education centers, and instructional technology. For the majority of tenured faculty, who are threatened today with stagnation as more and more instructors at colleges and universities become tenured, professional development must also bring renewal. It is essential in getting the faculty out of the ruts into which they have fallen in their teaching and suggesting new directions for growth in midlife (Lindquist, 1981).

Many tenured faculty can be especially interested in various challenges faced by institutions today, such as facilitating lifelong learning for students and implementing technology in new ways. Thus, the faculty will need to learn how to assess learning derived from extensive adult experience, then design curricula and programs to build on that learning. Faculty are also being encouraged to use new technology such as the Internet and World Wide Web to change the way that faculty research is evaluated (Wilson, 1998). These faculty should consider other new directions: helping today's students facilitate career and life transitions (which the faculty themselves may also be experiencing), improving conditions within the institution for teaching, managing multiple learning resources, and working with their junior colleagues. Mentoring by senior faculty is not new in higher education, but it is now recognized as holding great value not only for the faculty being mentored, but also for the senior faculty member (Luna and Cullen, 1995). The protégés become empowered through the assistance of a mentor, while the mentors themselves also feel renewed through the sharing of power and the advocacy of collegiality.

Collegiality, sharing, and personal development components can also be found in development practices such as growth contracts or faculty development plans (Boice, 1992). Growth contracts have been described as having senior tenured faculty coach new nontenured faculty in planning individualized contracts, which can include a profile of strengths and weaknesses, a scheme for addressing weaknesses, and a means of assessing progress, including an advisory committee. One example of this practice, designed around competitive grants for faculty who prepared reports, contains the following items: self-assessment, a statement of current roles, long-range projections, synthesis (compatibility of self-judged strengths and weaknesses), a profile, a draft of the annual development plan, and a way to share the plan with an advisory board (Gaff and Wilson, 1971). Despite the persistence of reports about campus efforts to initiate growth contracts, few such programs have survived (Boice, 1992). Faculty development plans are more widely used.

Until recently, the basic resources of higher education were a professor, a textbook, and a classroom (Lindquist, 1981). But these resources have been multiplied with the use of sophisticated educational software, television, videos, and the Internet. Tenured faculty may be understandably wary of some development strategies, fearing that a related evaluation component that involves technology may affect them negatively. "What is called development, growth and self-improvement today becomes the means by which decisions for institutional personnel management purposes are made tomorrow" (Rifkin, 1995, p. 2).

Faculty Development and Posttenure Review

Although many faculty development activities do produce data that can be used in faculty evaluations (such as posttenure review), few policies explicitly tie the two together (Aleamoni, 1990). The most compelling reason is probably the belief that few representative or truly accurate outcome measures rate the real effectiveness of students' learning, content material and organization, innovative teaching techniques, and student-teacher orientation. Some posttenure evaluation systems have a "trigger" effect, in which an evaluation of unsatisfactory performance results in the forced implementation of a faculty development plan. This process is different, however, from other institutions that require all faculty to complete development plans, regardless of their rank or tenure. The policy to create should be carefully considered, as the course to steer is a narrow one (Lunde and Healy, 1988). Faculty development committees or directors should not be directly involved in administering a reward system for the institution, but they can do other important functions—for example, conduct research and provide information on identifying qualities of effective teaching, validate standardized evaluation instruments, investigate the use of portfolios in documenting teaching activity, invite external consultants who are experts in faculty evaluation, and arrange for workshops that define teaching and scholarship at a particular institution.

Some faculty believe that even a formative posttenure review process that involves faculty development is a waste of time, because nothing comes of it (Chesky, 1997). This situation can happen if an institutional posttenure review policy does not have strong consequences or "teeth" for those who do not perform. The individual faculty development plan that results from such a system, while good in theory, may not be followed through and achieve the desired results. As stated, the AAUP recently published a statement with guidelines on posttenure review (American Association of University Professors, 1997; Leatherman, 1998). The standards state that posttenure review should be developmental, and, if they are linked to a formal faculty development program, the administration should not enforce the criteria unilaterally. A grievance procedure should also be available for both posttenure reviews and faculty development plans. These strategies would help assure participating faculty that the overall process is not a waste of time and that it does lead to effective results.

A study of performance evaluation of tenured faculty at 20 universities found two types of uses: (a) for salary recommendations and (b) formative or development strategies for tenured faculty (Reisman, 1986). The first type—a formal summative review primarily used in determining recommendations for annual salary—is the more commonly found evaluation. Tenured faculty are generally analyzed according to the same guidelines as nontenured faculty. The study describes the second type of performance evaluation as formative or developmental. This system provides a systematic review of the professor's performance with the goal to provide feedback for improving performance and clarifying future career directions. The study surveyed respondents from three universities with the focus on performance review and compared the results with respondents from six universities who focus more on salary reviews. The results found that developmental reviews are perceived as better in improving faculty teaching, research, and service than those performance evaluation systems that focus on salary reviews.

The relationship between posttenure review and faculty development is complex, and it can be viewed as two distinctive entities that, while different, are not mutually exclusive. An interesting view of posttenure review has two definitions, the second one of which has a development component:

- Post-Tenure Legalism: *The overt use of formal post-tenure review machinery and resultant documentation as an intentional, periodic trippet for subsequent due process pre-legal hearings that are designed to determine whether any tenured faculty member(s) should be dismissed either for cause or in accord with the existing financial exigency requirements of an institution. This legalistic approach does not preclude the primary use of post-tenure review for developmental purposes. . . .*
- Post-Tenure Developmentalism: *The disposition to utilize either formal or informal post-tenure review processes exclusively for faculty development and rewards-based purposes in a manner that precludes their advertent, catalytic use in providing grounds for potential dismissal cases.* (Felicetti, 1989, p. 51)

These definitions were used in a study of 28 Jesuit schools in which the chief academic officers were asked to provide their perspectives about their institution's current and anticipated posttenure review practices. The primary findings include the belief that while societal and judicial permission appear to exist for institutions to adopt posttenure legalism, the predominant orientation of posttenure review in the near future will be developmentalism. Building upon these definitions, another research study the following year offers a similar definition of posttenure evaluation: that the primary purpose of the evaluation is to ensure continued faculty vitality and development (Johnson, 1993). Two institutions were selected for the study, one a small 4-year liberal arts college and the other a large state university. Administrators, faculty, and staff were interviewed to determine whether posttenure faculty evaluation is a viable option for the revitalization and development of faculty. The findings indicate that while a system of posttenure review is not likely to reverse the problem of faculty who have become lax and unproductive, moderate improvements can be expected in their performance. The study also found evidence that enough dissatisfaction exists with current methods of evaluating tenured faculty to warrant further experimentation with posttenure review as a means for revitalization.

Summary

Development and improvement of tenured faculty have many ingredients. The work of organizational theorists has had an impact on some but not all the faculty development programs uncovered in this review. Some programs strive to address the periods of transition that faculty go through using posttenure developmentalism, while others take a more "Theory X" and "Theory Y" approach through posttenure legalisms. The literature reviewed in this section shows that faculty development often includes personal, instructional, organizational, and curricular components, and broadly develops faculty as professionals. Research shows that tenured faculty need and want to get involved but also need the proper support and encouragement. Overall, programs in higher education appear to be continually evolving and growing in addressing the needs of tenured faculty, which include the development of skills and knowledge using information technology, creating a shared vision of how faculty development can benefit all, keeping the needs of the individual and the institution in mind, and fostering continual lifelong and organizational learning. The next section examines some specific examples of posttenure faculty development at colleges and universities today that can be used as a basis for creating a system of improvement and appreciation.

POSTTENURE FACULTY DEVELOPMENT
IN ACTION

The literature reviewed so far on tenure, faculty development, and posttenure review reveals several principles upon which effective posttenure faculty development strategies should be based. These principles include using the significant expertise of tenured faculty available, combining summative and formative policies, understanding the stages or fluid cycles of discovery in faculty careers, and understanding the importance of the institutional mission and faculty-driven approaches. This section examines several examples of posttenure faculty development programs currently in use at different types of colleges and universities. These examples are classified as three types: optional, required, and jointly sponsored programs; they were selected based on the aforementioned principles. Many of the programs have won awards, are recognized as important through government grants received, or are noted in the education literature as having qualities that make their approaches worthy of further examination. The aging professoriat has valuable experience that should be tapped, produces more scholarly work, and, if properly developed, can be an invaluable resource to higher education today. Nevertheless, some obstacles need to be overcome—changing technology, the malaise of some tenured faculty, the lack of effective incentives for continued involvement and participation as tenured faculty progress in their career paths, for example. Development programs should take into account the concept of different career stages or the fluid cycle of discovery that many faculty experience in their careers to facilitate continued overall organizational learning.

In addition, ideal types of emphasis on faculty performance differ according to institutional type and mission (Baldridge, Curtis, Ecker, and Riley, 1978). Colleges that emphasize teaching and/or service as opposed to research need to concentrate more effort on faculty development policies that reinvigorate routine teaching and retrain faculty for changing curricular emphasis (Clark and others, 1990). The institutions that emphasize research and scholarly output need development and support for scholarly productivity. Tenured faculty in particular can be especially sensitive to matching faculty development policies with their campus missions and individual professional goals. Much of the literature that evaluates faculty

---

development programs collects information through site visits and through surveys of program coordinators, faculty members, and/or administrators (Centra, 1976; Eble and McKeachie, 1985; Gaff, 1978; Nelson and Siegel, 1980). The results usually show that the most successful faculty development approaches were indeed geared toward the type of institution and faculty that the practices served.

Examining the programs described in this section can be helpful to readers in considering potential strategies for tenured faculty at different types of institutions, professional associations, and university centers. A management improvement process called benchmarking that originated in business has recently become popular in higher education as a means of identifying and adapting best practices (Alstete, 1995). True benchmarking involves not only collecting secondary data and examples of best practices, but also examining firsthand how the best practices are achieved and finding ways to adapt them for improvement in the home institution. This process can be useful when looking at posttenure faculty development in other institutions to determine which practices are "best" and suitable to adapt to one's home college or university.

Optional Posttenure Faculty Development Programs

As noted, faculty development programs can be largely optional for tenured faculty or required as part of a posttenure review system. The optional programs specifically geared toward tenured faculty are often part of a comprehensive system of faculty development offerings. Larger institutions often have what can be described as "cafeteria" programs, which allow faculty to choose from a selection of services (Eble and McKeachie, 1985). Many recent Hesburgh Award winners and recipients of Certificates of Excellence are state-assisted 4-year institutions: Brooklyn College–City University of New York, Miami University, University of California–Santa Barbara, University of Maryland–Eastern Shore, University of Missouri–Columbia, University of South Carolina, and Virginia Tech (Teachers Insurance and Annuity Association/College Retirement Equities Fund, 1997, 1998). Brooklyn College's multifaceted faculty development program, Transformations, was introduced in 1994; it contains several features that are of special benefit to tenured faculty. The Freshman Year College at

Brooklyn combines block programming, accelerated summer programs, tutorial assistance, and faculty development strategies to facilitate the transition to college for new incoming students. Senior tenured faculty who were accustomed to teaching upper-division students are encouraged, through the core curriculum, to focus on ensuring success for the college's newest students. A component of Transformations is the appointment of Faculty Fellows, who coordinate the Freshman Year College's new block programs, expedite daily communication among block faculty and peer tutors, and serve as mentors to new faculty participating in the blocks. The success and impact of the Brooklyn College program is revealed in a study of student retention for the 1995 entering class, which shows a 74.7% student retention rate (a 50% improvement) after four semesters. This improvement resulted in a 17-credit increase in accumulation of credits, the equivalent of one full semester after three semesters (see Figure 4).

In addition, a survey of that faculty found that 84% were willing to teach in the freshman programs again. As of this writing, 110 senior and primarily tenured faculty had taught in the block programs. These types of faculty development strategies that are connected with other campus initiatives, such as the Freshman Studies program at Brooklyn College, can reinvigorate senior tenured faculty, improving their own

Faculty development strategies that are connected with other campus initiatives can reinvigorate senior tenured faculty.

FIGURE 4

Student Retention After 4 Semesters at Brooklyn College, City University of New York

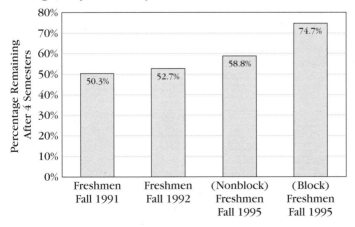

performance as well as that of their students. Placing tenured faculty back on the front line by teaching incoming freshmen reconnects these experienced scholars with the basic mission of the institution. This strategy supports many of the research articles previously cited that offer findings to support the importance of encouraging tenured faculty to share the vision of the institution through faculty and organizational development.

Miami University in Ohio also has a comprehensive and award-winning faculty development program that has components to stimulate tenured faculty (Cox, 1998). The Senior Faculty Program for Teaching Excellence was created to assist seasoned faculty in enhancing their interest and effectiveness in teaching; the program enables them to participate in a 2-semester experience of sharing in a community of scholars who value teaching, meeting for discussions, and pursuing individual teaching projects (Miami University, 1997, p. 39). Participants receive a 1-course reduction in their teaching assignment for one semester and $500 to support a teaching project. The 2 semesters of special activities are related to teaching and establish a forum for senior faculty from several disciplines to investigate many facets of teaching. The program is designed for faculty who have taught at Miami for at least 7 years; it was inspired by, but differs from, the Alumni Teaching Scholars Program (for junior faculty) in its format and expectations of participants. A booklet published by the Committee on the Improvement of Instruction and the Office for the Advancement of Scholarship and Teaching, *Teaching Grants, Programs, Resources, and Events, 1997-98,* states the goals of the Senior Faculty Program for Teaching Excellence:

- Honoring teaching as an intellectual pursuit
- Enhancing interest in teaching, teaching effectiveness, and student learning
- Advocating and developing educational and pedagogical innovation
- Understanding new disciplinary and interdisciplinary perspectives
- Interacting as an interdisciplinary community
- Integrating teaching and research into classroom experiences

- Using time and financial support for individual projects and investigations
- Discovering and incorporating ways that differences can enhance teaching and learning.

Each year, activities vary somewhat but are likely to include certain components:

- Discussions. *The group's seminars and roundtable settings focus on such topics as research in student learning, integrating teaching and research, introducing new technologies, videotaping teaching to enhance effectiveness, ethical dilemmas in teaching, teaching nontraditional students, and cooperative learning. Reading interest groups may emerge from the discussions.*
- National teaching conferences. *The Program funds the participants' attendance at Miami's Lilly Conference on College Teaching and another national conference such as Lilly-West, American Association for Higher Education, or American Association of Colleges and Universities.*
- Teaching projects. *Each participant designs and carries out a project for which he or she receives financial support of up to $500. Projects might include design of a capstone course or obtaining new expertise in a teaching technology or methodology. The project need not be fully designed before beginning to participate in the Program.*
- Writing. *The Programs provide an opportunity for participants to write papers, alone or together, on pedagogy in their disciplines or interdisciplinary fields. The Lilly Conference on College Teaching and the* Journal on Excellence in College Teaching *can provide a national forum for papers accepted for presentation or publication.*
- Teaching partnerships. *Pairs or groups of participants in the Program may form teaching partnerships in which members visit each other's classes and interview each other's students. The New Jersey "Partners in Learning" program has had success with similar exchanges.*
- Student consultants. *Each participant selects one or two students who provide [their] perspectives on the topics and practices covered in the program.* (Miami University, 1997, pp. 39–40)

The Miami program is a good example of how effective faculty development programs can be designed especially for senior tenured faculty. As noted earlier in the literature review, such faculty development methods can vary in their approach. Miami's strategy stretches across personal, curricular, instructional, and organizational development but focuses primarily on the institution's teaching goals. The goals of the faculty development program should be related to the institution's goals if the program is to succeed in developing tenured faculty. Tenured faculty, on the basis of their lifetime employment contract with the institution, often have an inherent need to feel that whatever kinds of development programs they participate in should be connected to the mission of the institution they chose to become tenured at.

Posttenure faculty development strategies are becoming more common elements of comprehensive faculty development efforts at colleges and universities. Indiana University Purdue University Indianapolis (IUPUI) has an Office of Faculty and Senior Staff Development in the Center for Teaching and Learning that was opened in 1994. The center exists to provide faculty with assistance in their quest for self-improvement by providing opportunities to explore new avenues of teaching; develop new courses or redesign existing ones; test new methods and delivery systems; create new ways to use technology to enrich teaching, research, and service; and encourage discussion and sharing of these methodologies (Indiana University, 1998).

Among the opportunities for tenured faculty is a workshop on proposal development and grant writing that was offered in summer 1998. Workshop participants met one day per week for six weeks from 9 A.M. to 4 P.M. Each session was led by Indiana University grant administration professionals and faculty who had written successful grant proposals. Topics covered included funding possibilities and strategies, basics of preparing a competitive proposal, proposal submission processes, compliance, and more. Participants worked full time on the preparation of an actual proposal during the fellowship period, completed special assignments, contacted funding agencies, met with faculty mentors, and proceeded toward resolution of specific problems. The participants met all requirements of the fellowship upon submission of a grant proposal to an external funding agency. The award consisted of a maximum of $6,000 for salary and/or expenses, not to exceed 20% of the previous fiscal year's salary, and no additional employment or stipend was allowed to be held concurrently. Eighty percent of the award was paid up front, the remaining 20% upon submission of the completed grant proposal. For faculty from campuses other than IUPUI, partial funding was to have been secured from the home campus, and the Office of Faculty and Senior Staff Development was available to assist in the process. These types of research/service opportunities are a valuable addition to teaching development strategies for tenured faculty at institutions such as Indiana University. They may place a higher importance on outside funding proposals and grant writing than some of the other institutions that offer posttenure faculty development programs. Posttenure faculty development should be mission driven.

Some colleges have teaching and research support funds for development that are open to all faculty but to which tenured faculty are given preference. For example, the College of Charleston has a Faculty Research and Development Committee comprising faculty charged with the responsibility to support and encourage faculty research and development (College of Charleston, 1996). The committee supports a wide range of professional activities that benefit the college and the professional development of its faculty. Individuals and groups are welcome to apply for projects including research, professional nondegree training, interdisciplinary learning, and work with professionals outside the college. Proposals leading to external funding and interdisciplinary proposals are also encouraged. Proposals for up to $2,500 may be submitted in several areas:

- *Faculty research* to help establish, maintain, and support scholarly and artistic activities and research projects;
- *Faculty development* to assist faculty in improving their professional skills or in developing new areas of expertise. Types of activities include but are not limited to short courses, workshops, colloquia, ACE fellowships, etc.;
- *Faculty professional support* to assist faculty in the dissemination of scholarly or artistic work. Types of activities include but are not limited to final preparation of manuscripts for publication, page costs for journal

articles, and shipping costs for art works in juried exhibitions. Normally, faculty professional support covers nontravel expenses; requests for supplementary travel expenses for participation in professional meetings should be directed to the department.

- *Continuous study grant* provides for full-time work on a research or development project conducted during a continuous 5-week period when not under contract to the college. Normally, this grant would be funded during the summer months. The dates for projects must be specified in the proposal.

Award holders may not accept supplementary employment during the term of the award, and they must remain on the college faculty in the academic year following the period of the award. Salary is included in the paycheck(s) and is treated as taxable income.

The idea of awarding preference to tenured faculty for this kind of extra support may seem wrong to those who are primarily concerned with attracting and retaining new faculty. Nevertheless, these policies may even act as incentives for new faculty to seek tenure at the institution and, of course, act as incentives for tenured faculty to continue their development and be rewarded for their seniority. In addition, from the administration's point of view, decisions about allocating funds should be based on defensible reasons on the need for posttenure faculty development.

Adequate funding is an important resource that can motivate and develop tenured faculty. Another institution that has such funds available is the University of Minnesota, which offers the Distinguished McKnight University Professorship Program (University of Minnesota, 1998). The professorships are made possible by a generous endowment from the McKnight Foundation to the university's graduate school in the mid-1980s and matched by a share of the permanent university funds for the purposes of supporting faculty development. Originally conceived as a career development plan for outstanding junior faculty, the program has been expanded to incorporate a program for distinguished midcareer faculty. The University places a great deal of importance on this special public/private partnership (University of Minnesota, 1998).

University administrators believe that the strength of a university lies in the quality and vitality of its faculty. To flourish, faculty members who have demonstrated a capacity for highly productive and creative work and who have a commitment to the university must be rewarded and recognized for their achievements. The University of Minnesota regards the Distinguished McKnight University Professorship as an important component of its university-wide faculty development programs. It complements the McKnight Land-Grant Professorship for outstanding junior faculty, the numerous endowed chairs created through the university's capital campaign in the 1980s, and the Regents Professorship for eminent senior faculty.

The goal of the Distinguished McKnight University Professorship Program is to honor and reward the university's highest achieving faculty who recently attained the status of full professor—especially those whose careers have advanced at Minnesota, whose work and reputation are identified with Minnesota, who bring renown and prestige to the university, and who can be expected to make additional significant contributions to their discipline in the future. Recipients are honored with the title "distinguished McKnight university professor," which they hold for as long as they remain at the University of Minnesota. The grant associated with the professorship consists of $100,000 over five years, to be used for research, scholarly, or artistic activities and expended at the recipient's discretion (University of Minnesota, 1998).

To select recipients each year, the graduate school invites each department to nominate its most outstanding faculty member to have recently achieved full professor status (in other words, within approximately 10 years). A committee of prominent faculty from across the university reviews the nominations (received by late December) and selects the winners, who are chosen for their scholarly or creative achievements and their potential for greater attainment, the distinction and honor they bring to the University of Minnesota, the quality of their teaching and advising, and their contributions to the wider community. The first 10 recipients of the award were chosen in spring 1996. In the future, 5 or 6 recipients will be named each year and presented to the Board of Regents in the late spring (University of Minnesota, 1998).

Programs for faculty renewal and development help individuals in several ways. They help interrupt the cycle of burnout for individuals, and they provide an enriched environment for growth and change (Chandler, 1988). Another fellowship program designed to foster opportunities for professional renewal for midcareer and late-career faculty is the Senior Teaching Fellows Program at the University of Georgia (University of Georgia, 1998). This program was established in 1988 through a 3-year grant from FIPSE. The program provides a means to focus the energies of a select group of senior faculty on lower-division undergraduate instruction. Each fellow receives a grant for an individual project to improve a specific undergraduate course or course sequence. In addition, fellows are encouraged to share their experience and expertise through mentoring relationships with junior faculty and teaching assistants.

Reforming and improving the curriculum is a widespread activity at colleges and universities today and an important focus of some faculty development programs. Programs such as the one at the University of Georgia can encourage and support tenured faculty to use their vast experience to guide changes in the curriculum that address today's trends, including changing technology, globalization, cultural pluralism, integration of knowledge, active learning, outcomes assessment, and more.

As noted, awards, fellowships, and paid leaves are common elements of strategies involving posttenure faculty development. The Office of Professional and Organizational Development at the University of Nebraska–Lincoln, Institute of Agricultural and Natural Resources (IANR), has a strategy for long-term posttenure development that includes faculty development leaves, the Academic Resource Network (faculty exchange), and a program called NUPROF (Office of Professional and Organizational Development, 1997a). NUPROF, originally a joint renewal and redirection program between the University of Nebraska and Minnesota Colleges of Agriculture, has been in operation since 1983 (Office of Professional and Organizational Development, 1997a). Until 1987, the program was targeted specifically to faculty with a teaching appointment. NUPROF has demonstrated the structure and flexibility to enhance professional and personal growth of faculty whatever their appointment, however, and is available to tenured faculty in IANR or to those who have been there 6 years or more. More than 200 faculty have participated in NUPROF (see Appendix B for the program description).

The NUPROF program is basically a guided process for developing, implementing, and funding an individual development plan for tenured faculty. The program provides an off-campus retreat for creation of a plan, funding up to $1,500, and a choice of avenues for growth. These avenues may include subject matter the faculty member desires to update, instructional methodology, new technology, or human relations. The program can provide needed structure for planned change and the opportunity to address changing institutional priorities. As noted, changing priorities of colleges and universities is a strong reason for creating programs that address the development needs of tenured faculty by appreciating their long service to the institution and offering opportunities for self-improvement.

Faculty leaves, as a component of the long-term development posttenure strategy at IANR, are designed to be a vehicle for accomplishing professional, personal, and organizational goals that a tenured faculty member would have difficulty achieving while undertaking the usual responsibilities (Office of Professional and Organizational Development, 1997c). The leaves can stress further academic study, renewal and redirection to a new role, or a total re-training program. No matter what the specific goal of the leave is for a faculty member, it should allow an opportunity to break the usual pattern and routine of faculty life (committees, extension service, research, and teaching assignments). A change in scenery and expectations can provide a perspective that will help renew senior faculty and provide a chance to formalize some professional "endings" and moving to new "beginnings" (Office of Professional and Organizational Development, 1997b). Leaves are limited to faculty who have held full-time appointments within the University of Nebraska for 6 years or more at the rank of assistant, associate, or full professor (or their equivalent).

The third component of the posttenure faculty development policy at IANR is the Academic Resource Network (Office of Professional and Organizational Development, 1997b). This component allows faculty to use ARNOLD©, a program of the Academic Resource Network in collaboration with Buffalo State College and the Research

Foundation of the State University of New York (ARNOLD, 1997). It is a free on-line service for individuals who would like to register and search for partners with whom to exchange data, do collaborative work, or share research. Individuals may also use ARNOLD© to search for positions posted by institutions. (See Appendix A for more information about this program.)

As stated, posttenure reviews at some institutions consist of annual reviews, which are short-term assessments and are often linked to merit pay (Lewis and Kristensen, 1997; Morreale and Licata, 1997). Although the posttenure review itself is required, the opportunity to seek merit pay may be optional. Community colleges, private colleges and universities, and large research universities have a variety of different types of merit pay or "merit reward" systems in place (Andrews, 1987). For example, the guidelines for merit pay at Southeast Missouri State University state that the primary mission of the "academy of scholars" is creating and sustaining an environment of lifelong learning and that such an environment exists where excellence in teaching is defined by discipline standards for the integration of scholarship and service with teaching and learning (Southeast, 1996). The intent of the guidelines is to establish the principles upon which a yearly appraisal system can be created by departments for the purpose of rewarding faculty who maintain high standards of teaching excellence as defined by the university's Teacher-Scholar Model.

Typically, salary increases awarded at institutions with merit pay are between $500 and $3000. Some colleges limit the percentage of faculty that will actually receive the awards, and many award policies are contingent upon the availability of funds. Merit recognition or merit pay in and of itself is not a complete answer to faculty development for tenured faculty, but it can motivate those professors who are attracted to monetary incentives. For some faculty, required periodic reviews with development requirements may be the best method for continuing their growth and learning. Merit pay can also be a valuable component of an overall strategy. For example, at King's College in Pennsylvania, where the faculty reward system has been redesigned (Farmer, 1993), the new system mixes intrinsic and extrinsic incentives in three interrelated institutional initiatives related to general educational reform, senior faculty performance appraisal, and merit pay.

An early result of the effort is a perceptible improvement in faculty members' motivation and productivity.

The optional posttenure faculty development programs reported and analyzed here have several common themes, including a link between institutional mission and faculty development, blended approaches, and encouragement of role rediscovery for tenured faculty. The institutions that believe teaching is their primary mission usually offer optional posttenure faculty development programs with an emphasis on teaching, whereas research-oriented institutions often offer programs aimed at supporting the solicitation of outside funding and grants. The link to the college or university mission is an important strategy to ensure a program's viability and success. Another common element in the optional programs is the blending of traditional faculty development approaches—personal, professional, curricular, and organizational development—into a more cohesive program for tenured faculty that addresses both individual and institutional needs. This element is related to the last common theme of these optional programs: role rediscovery for individual faculty. The optional posttenure faculty development programs uncovered here seem to support the concept that tenured faculty can and should be supported in rediscovering their teaching, research, and service roles within the institution and the community. Many observers believe these strategies are effective in increasing faculty performance, motivation, and quality of students' learning.

Required Posttenure Faculty Development

The other primary method for designing posttenure faculty development processes in colleges and universities is to make them part of a required posttenure evaluation system. This common approach varies in method of implementation among institutions (University of Texas, 1996). This approach has the advantage of institution-supported consequences for nonperformance by tenured faculty members. The procedures are usually stated in a faculty handbook, institutional administrative policy, or a state law. To facilitate continuing faculty development, each faculty member can be subject to comprehensive peer review and evaluation at least once every 5 to 7 years after the award of tenure. The scope of the faculty evaluation should be comprehensive, and the department chair or equivalent administrator often informs the faculty member, the dean of the college or school, and other appropriate administrative officers about the results of the evaluation.

These policies are often created to ensure thorough, fair, and comprehensive posttenure review, and to facilitate continued faculty development. Posttenure review can be structured as a device for administrative decision making, as it assists in directing appropriate resources for faculty development. These policies can enable funds to be requested to provide assistance for faculty in their professional development. The department is often responsible for posttenure review; overall, it is a process involving collegial peer review and evaluation. The posttenure evaluation can be conducted by appropriate peers within the institution, either departmental faculty or departmental faculty in combination with others. Accomplishments in teaching, research, creative activities, and service following the award of tenure are usually the focus of the review. External evidence of a faculty member's performance should be incorporated into the review. This evidence can include national awards, honors, offices in national or international academic and professional organizations, editorial functions for scholarly journals, publications in refereed journals, grant review statements, and invitations to regional, national, or international meetings or exhibitions.

If the faculty member under review or the evaluation committee so requests, the review may also include evaluations from persons external to the institution who have been selected from a list provided by the faculty member and the peer review group. The chair of the department or primary unit usually counsels the faculty member about updating his or her vita and the identification of supporting documentation to be submitted for the review, including identification of peers to evaluate the faculty member's performance. The faculty member, in consultation with the chair of the department, should compile all documents to be submitted for review and forward them to the evaluation committee. These documents should include:

1. The current curriculum vita;
2. A letter of evaluation from the chairs of the primary unit;

3. Letters of evaluation from peers on campus;
4. A summary of student teaching evaluations as well as other indicators of teaching performance prepared by the chair of the primary unit;
5. Sample publications or creative works; and
6. Other materials deemed appropriate.

The faculty member, in consultation with the chair of the department, should request faculty peers on campus to submit evaluation letters. These letters, forwarded to the chair of the primary unit, should focus on accomplishments in teaching, research or creative work, and service since the award of tenure. The dean can then appoint a posttenure review committee. The dean should determine the composition of this committee after consultation with the chair of the primary unit and the faculty being reviewed each year. This committee has several duties:

1. To review all materials submitted on behalf of faculty members being reviewed and identify additional materials (if any) needed to complete the review;
2. To notify the appropriate primary unit chair of additional materials required to complete the evaluation and when such materials should be submitted, which may include soliciting additional letters of evaluation from on or off campus;
3. To conduct a comprehensive evaluation of faculty members' continued performance and accomplishments following the award of tenure;
4. To prepare a written summary for each faculty member that assesses faculty performance and, if appropriate, propose a development plan; and
5. To forward all written summaries to the chair of the department and to the faculty member for review.

The outcome of the review can be a summary statement on the evaluation developed by the department chair and, if appropriate, a written plan for the faculty member's development. The development plan should be written by the head of the primary unit in consultation with the faculty member. The department chair will work with the faculty member to achieve the objectives of the plan. As stated elsewhere in the literature on effective faculty development, department chairs are critical to the process of posttenure faculty development, for both required and optional programs.

The faculty development plan should include certain elements:

1. Teaching, research, and service goals for the planning period, including how the plan relates to departmental development efforts and plans and specific time frames for achieving various elements of the plan;
2. Resources viewed as critical to implementation of the plan; and
3. Actions proposed by the department to achieve successful completion of the plan.

The faculty development plan is intended to serve as a mechanism for assisting faculty in focusing their efforts and identifying appropriate ways in which resources can be directed to maximize development activities. Any faculty member who feels aggrieved by the posttenure review process can submit to the review committee any additional materials relevant to the evaluation or may appear before the review committee to present information, and may present materials relevant to the committee's deliberations or final evaluation. Finally, the review summary and the faculty development plan are submitted to the appropriate dean and senior administrator(s), who can review the results of the evaluation and the faculty member's plans to ensure compliance with the procedures. Normal institutional procedures should be made available to any faculty member who feels aggrieved by the posttenure review process as applied to him or herself (University of Colorado, 1997).

This type of highly structured and "triggered" approach to faculty development within posttenure review is becoming more common at colleges and universities. Some institutions structure their policy so that the posttenure review and development component are also available upon request by the faculty member. For example, Texas A&M University's policy, which is generally similar to others, also states that "a tenured faculty member desirous of the counsel of a professional review committee in evaluating his or her career may request such counsel by making a request to the department head" (Texas A&M, 1998, p. 1). This opportunity for a tenured professor to voluntarily request a review, in a system of required reviews, is a good way to encourage development activities and to show that the main objective of these posttenure systems is to *develop* faculty and not remove them. Tenured faculty may naturally become defensive when posttenure review policies are first discussed and implemented. One of the most important ideas to communicate is that the primary goal of these policies is to support and require the continuing growth of educated professionals, not to attack the tenure system.

Jointly Sponsored Development Programs Available to Tenured Faculty

Some institutions that require posttenure review with a faculty development component also offer their faculty the opportunity to participate in the optional program types described earlier. Colleges and universities also work cooperatively with each other through self-created collaborations (Wylie, 1990), professional associations, and faculty development programs sponsored by on-campus institutes and centers that are open to others (New Jersey, 1996). These kinds of jointly sponsored programs can be cost-effective for individual institutions, and facilitate important, useful, and enjoyable interinstitutional interaction by tenured and other faculty. For example, the New Jersey Institute for Collegiate Teaching and Learning (NJICTL) was founded in 1989 by the New Jersey Board of Higher Education to improve the quality of teaching and learning on the state's 56 campuses, both public and independent. It is located on the campus of Seton Hall University in South Orange, New Jersey. As one of two such state-wide programs in the nation, NJICTL has become a nationally recognized pioneer in multi-institutional approaches to faculty and instructional development. It is funded by the state of New Jersey, Seton Hall University, and national grants and funding agencies.

NJICTL was initially governed by an 11-member board of governors, including college trustees, presidents, and members of the New Jersey Board of Higher Education. In 1994, following the new governor's dissolution of the Board of Higher Education, NJICTL continued its state-wide service through sponsorship of a consortium called the Partnership for College Teaching, which is governed by a council of member campuses and supported in part by dues

The primary goal of review policies is to support and require the continuing growth of educated professionals, not to attack the tenure system.

from members. Programs and services offered include Faculty College, an exchange program for New Jersey faculty, a series of seminars, workshops, and consultation services to promote vitality among senior faculty (Partnership for College Teaching, 1996).

Another important multi-institutional vehicle for faculty development is the Washington Center for Improving the Quality of Undergraduate Education at Evergreen State College (Evergreen State College, 1999). Also known as Washington Center, it is a consortium of 46 colleges and universities based at Evergreen State College in Olympia. The center works at the grassroots level with faculty members and administrators to share expertise and carry out collaborative projects to improve undergraduate education in Washington. Through workshops, conferences, publications, and technical assistance, the Washington Center has stimulated a state-wide dialogue and has launched a number of initiatives related to collaborative teaching and learning, the reform of mathematics and science teaching, and cultural pluralism.

Washington Center grew out of a curriculum development and faculty exchange partnership between Evergreen State and Seattle Central Community College that began in 1984. Almost immediately, the partnership led to the idea of creating a wider network of campuses working on educational improvement. Grants from the Exxon and Ford Foundations officially launched the center in fall 1985. Since 1987, the Washington state legislature has allocated modest operating funds to the center as a public service initiative of Evergreen State. To carry out special projects, the center has raised additional funds from the Ford Foundation, the National Science Foundation, Burlington Northern, Seattle Pacific Bank, and the Boeing Company.

As stated, the Bush Foundation offers support for multi-institution faculty development programs. The foundation was established by Mr. and Mrs. Archibald Granville Bush of St. Paul, Minnesota, in 1953 to encourage and promote charitable, scientific, literary, and educational efforts. The foundation's major interest is on projects originating in Minnesota, North Dakota, and South Dakota. The foundation supports education at all levels, with an emphasis on higher education. Recently, most of the foundation's grants for higher education have been in specific, predefined areas, including assisting private colleges with matching grants and grants for faculty development at private and public colleges. The focus of the Bush Foundation's educational program is on the improvement of students' learning through the improvement of teaching and faculty development (Eble and McKeachie, 1985; Postema, 1999).

Most of the jointly sponsored faculty development programs reported here are open to both tenured and nontenured faculty. They occasionally cover several of the traditional development topics but usually focus on instructional and organizational development. Therefore, these jointly sponsored programs should not be relied on to cover all posttenure faculty development needs. As part of an overall strategy that combines internally developed optional programs and a separate posttenure review process, jointly sponsored programs can be a beneficial enhancement to posttenure development programs. Highly experienced tenured faculty who may have been at one institution for a very long time can especially benefit from interaction with colleagues from other institutions as they strive to develop themselves personally and professionally.

Other examples of seminars for faculty development sponsored by one institution but open to all include the Faculty Development in International Business seminars sponsored by the College of Business Administration at the University of South Carolina, seminars for faculty development in international business sponsored by the Robert Wang Center for International Business at the University of Memphis, and the faculty development programs at the Center for International Business and Education and Research/Institute for International Business, College of Business and Administration at the University of Colorado at Denver. These three programs are designed for faculty who want to add international content to their courses and/or develop new international courses. As the curricula of many colleges and universities address the issues of globalization, these kinds of international programs can offer beneficial development for tenured faculty who may need to update their international knowledge base.

Summary
This section has examined several optional and required development practices for tenured faculty, as well as several jointly sponsored programs. Faculty development programs

should match the institution's mission so that tenured faculty, who are most connected with the institution's long-term goals and success of the mission, can feel that programs are appropriate and more closely match their own objectives. It is also important that posttenure faculty development programs, whether required, optional, or jointly sponsored by several institutions, measure outcomes for continuous improvement. One method suggested for measuring a program's success involves the use of benchmarking, which seeks to identify best practices by comparing performance with other programs. Optional programs, merit pay, and posttenure review with a development component all offer potential answers to the challenge of developing tenured faculty. After reviewing the various possible approaches, the author of this monograph believes in a largely optional approach for true development programs to be successful. It is more difficult for faculty to plan for significantly higher performance if they believe that their pay, and perhaps continued employment, are contingent on what they write in an annual development plan. Monitoring required performance of tenured faculty has a place in the overall management of faculty, such as a separate posttenure review process that is required periodically and has consequences for tenured professors who do not meet even the basic requirements for acceptable teaching, scholarship, and service. Administrators and faculty developers may now seek to learn some practical advice for designing and implementing effective faculty development programs.

DESIGNING DEVELOPMENT PROGRAMS FOR TENURED FACULTY

At a time when some resources for higher education are becoming limited by states and the Federal Government and institutions are being pressured to produce more results, tenured faculty members are a valuable resource that needs to be developed and nurtured to help address these concerns. So far, this report has explored related literature on the need for posttenure faculty development and reviewed examples of how to develop and nurture tenured faculty at colleges and universities. But what organizational model should be adapted and what specific recommendations can be learned from the research and examples uncovered for establishing posttenure development programs and monitoring their effectiveness?

Overall, an institution's philosophy and mission should provide the framework for posttenure review and faculty development policy. Based on this mission-driven philosophy, the faculty development literature, and the examples discussed in this monograph, a general model of posttenure faculty development in higher education today is proposed in Figure 5. External changes affecting the internal environment of institutions that particularly influence faculty development programs include new instructional and information technology, student and faculty demographics, public perceptions about tenure, state legislation, and accreditation requirements. An analysis of the literature and examples in this report finds that development programs for tenured faculty can be classified as required, optional, or jointly sponsored. Effective posttenure faculty development should consist of separate optional and required elements, with instructional, personal, curricular, and organizational development components. These components are largely aimed at the outcomes of teaching, scholarship, service, and student learning. Faculty should be offered appropriate rewards for continuous, lifelong development and negative consequences for failure to grow and change with the needs of the students, the institution, and the society higher education serves. As with many processes in higher education, it is important that development of tenured faculty be guided by the mission and that the outcomes be evaluated for continuous evaluation and review. Methods of evaluation involve various assessment methods, benchmarking, feedback from alumni, external ratings by third parties, enrollment, self-evaluation, and other

FIGURE 5

Posttenure Faculty Development Model

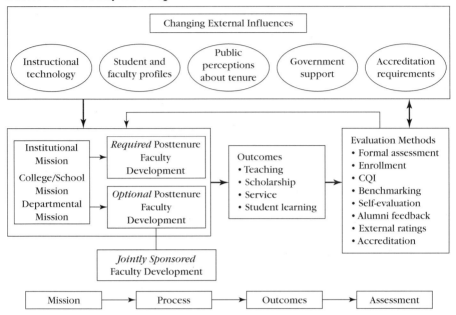

procedures. The data from these evaluation methods flow both to and from the external environment, yielding changes in how faculty are valued internally and by the world outside higher education. Few institutions today have a truly comprehensive system of posttenure faculty development such as that contained in this model. Certain areas need further refinement at many colleges and universities, for example, the effective design of required posttenure faculty development policies to ensure more than minimal performance, a clearly defined set of optional and required programs, and a wider variety of programs. Tenured faculty need a choice of programs to help them develop their instructional, curricular, organizational, and personal abilities.

Recommendations and Tools for Effective Program Development

It has been suggested that interaction with like-minded peers, periodic changes in the nature of the work or the work setting, and administrative and organizational intervention are important strategies for helping senior faculty members stay interested and productive (Finkelstein and Jemmott, 1993). A study involving in-depth interviews of 20 university professors at midlife listed the participants' suggestions that they believed would contribute to improving emotional and work-related aspects of academic life for tenured faculty (Karpiak, 1997). They included the belief that institutional administration should:

- Provide academic support and resources for research, including space to carry out research and time, through lower teaching loads;
- Communicate to the public through the media the valuable contributions of faculty and support staff and defend its members more vigorously before the public;
- Promote among faculty a sense that they are involved in a joint enterprise and that they are members of a team;
- Foster an environment in which colleagues stimulate each other's intellectual interests and help each other to grow as intellectuals; and
- Develop support networks.

Research on faculty development activities at different institutions has found that the most frequently tried approach to faculty development and the approach that yielded the highest success rate was professional development (Nelson and Siegel, 1980). This approach includes conventional activities such as study leaves, attendance at professional meetings, and research and publication activities in a faculty member's discipline, all of which can be relevant to tenured faculty.

Tenured faculty, however, may find collective approaches to faculty development, such as campus-wide activities or intercampus programs, especially attractive because they enable them to break out of the routine and work with other colleagues. Some of the early research found that the more successful programs were characterized by effective management and that management of the program was even more critical for the success of faculty development than general management of the institution (Nelson and Siegel, 1980). Components of effective management were found to include a clearly structured decision-making unit (either a faculty committee or a group of top administrators), communication of the relationship between faculty development activities and the institution's reward structure, and the ability of decision making to be flexible with regard to authorizing various different strategies for faculty development.

Faculty development programs are more successful if they seek out the participation of and input from a variety of faculty members and consult faculty in planning decisions (Licata, 1986; Nelson and Siegel, 1980; Sorcinelli, 1988). The administration and faculty leaders should then clearly define the objectives of the program and what kinds of development (professional, instructional, curricular, organizational) will be emphasized. The potentially important role of the department head is often a neglected dimension in faculty development programs (Lucas, 1988; Moore, 1986; Nelson and Siegel, 1980). Chairs are the key to faculty development, because they read the course evaluations, prepare faculty development plans, and handle complaints from students (Moscato, 1998). It is believed that if one department poorly develops its faculty, then it can negatively influence the management of other departments as well. A research study of 311 chairs at eight midwestern public universities was conducted to assess chairs' perceptions of administrative and faculty development, and their degree of participation in development activities and roles (Bowman, 1991). The findings indicate that although chairs view both administrative development and faculty development as important, faculty development is judged as more important. Chairs reported spending 10% to 15% of their time performing various faculty development roles, such as assisting faculty to obtain resources and improving faculty research and teaching. Institutions seeking to promote development among their administrators need to encourage such activities vigorously, provide incentives, and present such activities locally.

The issue of individual department activities versus institution-wide faculty development programs has been discussed in the literature (see, e.g., Licata and Morreale, 1997; Nelson, 1979; Vazulik and Sullivan, 1986), and the idea of a balanced approach that takes into account the broader institutional goals with departmental/curricular concerns is probably most valid. Faculty development must be flexible to meet individual situations (such as the needs of tenured faculty), but at times faculty must be guided into programs where institutional needs can be addressed. The overriding development of and guidance by the faculty should be kept paramount, however. By involving faculty members in the planning and encouraging them to be a part of the administration of the program, the ownership builds commitment and a sense of responsibility for and to the program (Redditt and Hamilton, 1978; Stordahl, 1981). Other practical hints for building the faculty's ownership of the programs and activities include:

A. Establish a "faculty advisory board" to provide input for the creation of [the] program and activities.

B. Utilize faculty committees to award grants and other competitive prizes.

C. Encourage institutional administrators (i.e., deans, provost, president) to maintain a low-profile image. The faculty development program needs to be perceived as being of, for, and by the faculty. Faculty development is concerned with faculty effectiveness, and many faculty assume institutional administrators are concerned with faculty efficiency.

D. Make use of "local talent" on your campus in staffing programs. Most research institutions can take pride in the number of faculty and staff who have the expertise and ability to offer various kinds of professional growth experiences to their colleagues. A seminar on "Strategies for Getting Published," for example, might best be conducted by internal faculty who are highly respected for their "publication list" by their colleagues on campus. Using campus faculty to teach campus faculty promotes collegiality.

E. Involve the department chairperson in the planning and running of faculty development activities to the highest extent possible. The department chairperson is the "front line" in faculty development; he or she works most closely with department colleagues and can best ascertain their needs and wants, their moods, the variety of pressures . . . they are feeling, etc. (Altman, 1986, p. 53)

Tenured faculty should be included on the advisory board and other committees to make sure the needs of the senior faculty are addressed. Moreover, the "local talent" mentioned earlier could consist of highly respected tenured faculty, who might feel honored to be asked to conduct a workshop for their colleagues.

Involving the faculty is just one factor to consider when planning development programs. In addition to the issue of the faculty's involvement, other aspects are important for successful faculty development programs, including providing an acceptable rationale to the faculty, voluntary participation, flexibility in programming, rewards for participation, careful scheduling and continuity for the program, proper publicity for the program, adequate funding, and critical nonmonetary support from the upper administration (Hammons and Wallace, 1976). Program designers should be aware that no panacea, no cure-all, exists for the ills of the institution's instructional staff and that each college and university should address solutions individually (Stordahl, 1981). Obstacles to overcome in implementing a program may include administrators' apathy, resistance from the faculty, and, some believe, the lack of a link to an evaluation system. As noted, the concept of linkage has both pros and cons. Some institutions and educational systems choose to create optional posttenure faculty development programs, while others implement them as part of required, formalized posttenure review. Institutions that opt for linkage should involve legal counsel in setting such policy (Baez and Centra, 1995). Moreover, institutions should conduct the reviews annually and establish grievance procedures that are simple to follow.

Tenured faculty should also be involved in the appointment of, and are usually the strongest candidates for, those who wish to serve as a chief faculty developer within an institution. The three common staffing patterns include full-time staff members specifically hired for the positions, faculty members with joint appointments in academic units who work part-time at the center, or graduate students who work part-time at the center (Sell and Chism, 1991). Each arrangement has several advantages and disadvantages, many of them self-evident, with regard to areas such as stability and continuity, commitment, status within the institution, knowledge base with regard to teaching, knowledge base with regard to development of teachers, complement of staff, and personnel costs. The position of director of faculty development, or its equivalent, can be used in the primary areas of responsibility for faculty development: personal, instructional, and organizational. Faculty developers can also serve as "change agents" in areas such as institutional reward structures and in-house funding systems (Zahorski, 1993). It is recommended that the position of director be established on a release-time basis for faculty, as opposed to having the leadership come from a committee structure. This approach enables an individual to have more leadership for change, responsibility, and accountability, and less diffusion of authority. The director should create the faculty advisory committee, however, to achieve the goal of broad faculty involvement. Leaders of faculty development should also:

- Seek and nurture both faculty and administrative support;
- Study all aspects of the institution, such as the culture, academic programs, committee system, administrative hierarchy, and organizational structure;
- Establish a willingness to serve and earn the respect of colleagues;
- Devise strategies for making the faculty development program more visible;
- Publish a faculty development newsletter;
- Develop a holistic program that offers a wide variety of activities, instruments, and programs;
- Maintain a nonpolitical stance and neutrality on many campus issues to avoid divisiveness and ill will, and to maintain constituencies (Zahorski, 1993).

Because the largest faculty constituency is the tenured group, it is important to design programs and activities especially suited for it. Optional programs can be designed as part of an overall plan for faculty development. A grid can be created to help set up, map, and conceptualize faculty development activities for faculty at different stages of their careers and to ensure that multiple roles are supported (see Figure 6).

The grid can help address the needs of tenured faculty, particularly in Rows 2 and 3. In addition, Row 4 lists resources that help faculty with all three mission areas and with balancing work roles and personal roles. For example, programs aimed at tenured faculty, such as NUPROF or the Senior Teaching Fellows Program, may be listed on

FIGURE 6

Framework for Mapping Faculty Development Resources

Resources to Support Faculty Roles Institutional Missions			
Resources for faculty career stages	**Column A** *Teaching*	**Column B** *Research*	**Column C** *Public service/ outreach*	**Column D** *Integrated roles*
Row 1: Early career				
Row 2: Midcareer				
Row 3: Late career				
Row 4: Resources for all career stages				

Instructions: Within each cell, list available resources and the unit providing each resource. In Column A, list resources specifically pertaining to the Teaching role; in Column B, resources pertaining to the Research role; in Column C, resources pertaining to the Public Service/Outreach role; in Column D, resources that assist faculty with all three roles and with balancing work and personal roles.

In Row 1, list resources specifically for early career faculty; in Row 2, resources for midcareer faculty; in Row 3, resources for late career faculty; in Row 4, resources for faculty at all career stages.

Source: Austin, Brocato, and Rohrer, 1997, p. 16. Used with permission.

Rows 2 and 3, while seminars on time management or research grants may benefit faculty across the ranks. The grid offers a background on which faculty developers can list the different developmental offerings available throughout the institution, highlighting those faculty career stages where additional resources are needed (Austin, Brocato, and Rohrer, 1997). Most of the structural advice on faculty development in the literature recommends the creation of a set of resources that support faculty in the full array of multiple roles they are expected to fulfill at the institution. Those institutions that emphasize teaching can place more emphasis on instructional faculty development resources, and research institutions can emphasize resources more central to their mission.

A survey of 195 randomly selected faculty developers from research, doctorate-granting, and comprehensive universities, and liberal arts colleges (Rubino, 1994) found that research and doctorate-granting universities consider instructional and research development programs to be of equal importance, that research universities offer instructional development programs most frequently, and that doctorate-granting universities offer organizational development programs most frequently. Comprehensive universities consider instructional and curriculum development programs to be of equal importance but offer personal development programs (such as career development) most frequently. Another study found that priorities changed at research institutions during the 1990s (Diamond and Adam, 1998). In a report presenting the findings of a 1996–97 survey of 11 research and doctoral institutions to determine how faculty, department chairs, and academic deans perceive the balance between research and undergraduate teaching at their institutions (which the institutions had also responded to 5 years earlier as part of a larger study of 49 institutions), the researchers found (a) overall, a stronger support for a balance between teaching and research than in the earlier survey; (b) a perception that institutions are placing greater importance on teaching than earlier; (c) a decline in the number of respondents reporting a strong personal emphasis on research; (d) changing criteria in the selection of faculty and department chairs toward a greater emphasis on teaching; and (e) differences among disciplines in perceptions about the appropriate balance between teaching and research. Open-ended comments often noted, however, that while institutional rhetoric had changed, policies and practices for promotions, tenure, and merit pay continue to reward research over undergraduate teaching and that resources continue to be allocated disproportionately to research activities.

The different roles that faculty should perform and the different stages in their careers should also be made clear at those institutions that choose to make posttenure development part of a formal posttenure review process. The faculty development plan is one of the key elements of systems to properly administer this clarification. Several business schools have policies that reflect this approach, among them the University of Wisconsin–Madison, the Milwaukee School of Business, and the Whitewater School of Business (Morreale and Licata, 1997). These institutions require professors to outline future development activities within the context of department, unit, and campus needs. These development plans, put into the posttenure review process, require that individuals prepare, discuss, and act upon retrospective and prospective professional development self-evaluations. Posttenure review guidelines also can have specific expectations for senior tenured faculty. For example, the Periodic In-depth Review Statement of the Department of Accounting at the University of Texas–Austin and the Guidelines for Periodic Evaluation of Tenured Faculty of the University of Texas state that each member of the accounting faculty will be evaluated every three years and will provide a personal statement describing research, education, and service activities (Morreale and Licata, 1997). Expectations for Faculty Ranks lists the expectations for assistant professors, associate professors, and full professors for the three areas. In the area of research, full professors are expected to have active research "streams" (p. 69) that include publications in journals recognized as leading in their field, and their contributions should be seen or recognized by colleagues throughout the field as central to the development of the field. They should also be known as one of the top people in their area of expertise. In the area of education, full professors are expected to have at least average teaching ratings when compared with instructors for all sections of that course and all sections of other courses of the same type. They are also expected to develop and successfully offer an elective course for graduate programs, work with doctoral students, and regularly chair dissertation committees. Expectations for internal service include membership on the departmental executive committee or other committees in the school and university. Full professors are expected to serve external constituencies in areas such as membership on editorial review boards of respected journals and to serve on national committees. Because the Accounting Department is in a professional school, full professors are also expected to demonstrate the ability to facilitate constructive interaction with practitioners relevant to their research and educational activities (Morreale and Licata, 1997). Many colleges and universities with a posttenure review system use such expectations as a basis for "triggering" a posttenure faculty development plan.

Some schools without formal posttenure review processes but whose faculty are mostly tenured also require all faculty to complete development plans. For example, the Hagan School of Business at Iona College requires that all faculty complete a development plan each year and submit it to their department chair. The Hagan School has 32 tenured faculty out of 38 total (84%), and so this planning process can be viewed as a large component of posttenure faculty development. Before the start of each academic year, faculty are sent the guidelines listed in Appendix C. Faculty are directed to examine their previous year's plan for accomplishments that were achieved and any possible areas for improvement. The guidelines then require faculty to write their goals in three areas: teaching and student learning; intellectual contributions and professional development; and service. A faculty committee and the dean review the planning process itself each year for continuous improvement.

The Faculty Development Research Initiative, outlined in the guidelines of the Hagan School of Business at Iona College, is a policy designed to increase intellectual activity in the form of refereed publications from all faculty. Under this policy, tenured faculty who have been through the tenure process and who may feel less motivated to publish are now rewarded with an additional incentive program that can award them up to a maximum of $3,900 per year. This award policy consists of up to 3 separate awards, and it is structured to support the teaching mission of the business school at Iona. Faculty are offered a greater dollar amount for peda-gogical-type articles ($1,200 each), and a slightly smaller amount for applied and basic research-type articles ($1,000 each). The faculty also receive rewards for up to three journal articles submitted ($100 each) each academic year. This pol-icy has helped increase the research output of refereed arti-cles to record levels at the school, as well as increase faculty members' satisfaction with the development process.

In addition to effective leadership and incentives, it is also good advice for faculty development programs and directors to position themselves as resource centers within the institution (Farr, 1988). Staff members are a major resource within a development center or office, and, as noted, it is desirable to have a full-time professional staff if funding permits. At larger institutions, consultation staff members should have a wide variety of backgrounds and expertise related to personal and career development, instruction, curriculum design, and research. Smaller institutions and/or those with less funding can draw associates from the faculty for short terms to offer expertise in areas such as lecture management, formative evaluation, grant writing, computer skills, and instructional technology. A faculty development program is also a good resource center for faculty members seeking colleagues for networking opportunities. New faculty can connect with tenured faculty through staff referrals and develop professional relationships to facilitate mentoring and research. Centers can offer electronic "carrots" in the development office to entice faculty into one-on-one interactions (Farr, 1988). Many faculty, especially some senior tenured faculty, may need extra help with computers or new teaching technology, and this method can show them the full range of services the office can provide.

The services offered tenured faculty do not have to be very expensive, and several tips are available for low-budget faculty development programs (Lang and Conner, 1988). The most popular recommendations in the literature involve conducting needs assessments, making a special effort to have administrative support for the program visible, and repeatedly emphasizing the grassroots nature of the planning process. Workshops with faculty making the presentations are usually lower in cost than hiring an outside speaker. If an outside speaker is highly desirable, costs can be cut by collaborating with other departments in the institution or other nearby colleges and universities. In addition to the formal workshops and presentations, faculty consultation programs by senior tenured faculty are a useful complement to other group activities. For example, the Office of Faculty Development in the School of Science and Engineering Careers, National Institute for the Deaf, and the Rochester Institute of Technology have had faculty sign up for assistance in developing skills ranging from questioning strategies in the classroom to developing valid tests (Lang and Conner, 1988). Many of the faculty in such professional schools are from business and industry and therefore have had little formal training in teaching and curriculum development. These kinds of faculty development offerings are especially beneficial to them. Often, both

Faculty consultation programs by senior tenured faculty are a useful complement to other group activities.

tenured and nontenured faculty can find benefits in simply communicating about perspectives on teaching one on one with a person outside their specialized discipline.

Open and honest faculty group discussions about the profession of teaching that meet regularly with support from institutions are often called "teaching circles" (Bernstein, 1986; Professional, 1995; Stephen, 1998; University of Nebraska, 1998; University of Oregon, 1998). Teaching circles can be found at a variety of different types of institutions, including Montclair State University in New Jersey, the University of Oregon, the University of Nebraska, Stephen F. Austin State University in Texas, and Iona College. They usually consist of groups of instructors who meet regularly to discuss teaching. The groups can operate as formally or informally as they wish, and they can take a variety of forms. For example, some teaching circles are unstructured, with the topic for discussion being whatever is on people's minds on that day. Others identify a series of topics they wish to discuss and work their way through the list. Some operate within a department or faculty, while others are cross-disciplinary. Some focus on a single topic for a term, while others discuss a new topic each week. Members of the circle usually make the decisions about the way the group operates and the frequency of meeting. Members of teaching circles can

- . . . *Take turns leading a discussion, with the topic selected by that meeting's leader;*
- . . . *Work their way through a book on teaching, or discuss a series of articles on teaching;*
- *[Review books];*
- . . . *Invite speakers, followed by discussion;*
- . . . *Reflect on and share their personal experiences in teaching;*
- *[Hear] reports from colleagues who went to a conference;*
- *Review potential classroom material together (presumes same discipline);*
- *Visit each other's classes and give feedback, or visit only to gain appreciation of other teaching situations;*
- *Invite students to meet with [the] group and give their views on teaching.* (University of Oregon, 1998, p. 1)

At the University of North Carolina at Asheville, the teaching circles program was started 4 or 5 years ago by the

University Teaching Council, a group of faculty members who had a small amount of money at their disposal to encourage discussions about development and encouragement of good teaching. Usually 1 or 2 people propose a circle, which then will have 4 to 10 members; they meet regularly, often over food, for discussions. They require some sort of dissemination at the end of the cycle. Toward the end of the 1990s, following some suggestions by colleagues in the social sciences, a teaching circle was organized on Teaching Literature Across the Disciplines. The circle had 10 members, representing the departments of literature, computer science, biology, physics, economics, political sciences, psychology, and sociology. At the end of the year, the circle produced a 10-page pamphlet on the topic. Other circles have discussed The Body, Promoting Effective Discussions, and Use of Oral Presentations in Management. Some are about a topic, others about a practice. They are usually but not always interdisciplinary. The grant for a teaching circle is usually between $500 and $1,000 and can include modest stipends, guest speakers, books, and other materials (University of Oregon, 1998). At the Hagan School of Business at Iona College, the teaching circle was started and is led by the two most senior faculty (both tenured); it meets monthly throughout the academic year to discuss a variety of topics about the school's primary mission—teaching.

Although strong funding for faculty development activities is not absolutely essential for success, faculty developers at state-assisted colleges and universities agree that more offerings will occur with additional funding (Raufman, 1991). A research study of California community colleges found that the programs' success and effectiveness are more closely associated with several characteristics: (a) a history of commitment to faculty development; (b) a shared vision by all that faculty development fosters organizational development; (c) program administrators with sufficient time and funding; (d) program goals related to institutional goals; (e) an organizational structure jointly satisfying both college and individual needs; and (f) effective procedures for communication, feedback, and change. An effective faculty development program can be designed to help both those faculty who are having trouble with an immediate teaching or research problem and whose who need general assistance in performing their faculty duties. Another study of publicly funded community colleges explored the lack of vitality among midcareer faculty (Kelly, 1990), examining the problems of midcareer faculty in terms of an impending shortage of faculty, symptoms of burnout, measures of vitality, and the specific concern about faculty vitality in the community college. The circle also examined institutional causes of the problem, paying particular attention to the campus culture, the departmental climate, the influences of colleagues, faculty workload, changes in student population, the tenure system, and the reward structure. Members offered suggestions for posttenure development of midcareer faculty that included individualized growth plans, career planning, faculty exchanges, faculty internships, sabbaticals, more variety in jobs, faculty development programs, posttenure evaluations, and incentives and rewards (Kelly, 1990).

Assessment of Posttenure Faculty Development Programs

Once the initial strategies and processes for posttenure faculty development are in place, often as part of a broader plan for all faculty, it is important to continually monitor the success of the programs and make adjustments accordingly. Research findings indicate that colleges and universities evaluate faculty development practices by measuring participants' satisfaction, the effects of the practices on the organization, on-the-job behaviors, and participants' learning (Rubino, 1994). One method of collecting information about participants' satisfaction is through structured surveys and comparative benchmarking. Educational Benchmarking Inc. (EBI) and the American Assembly of Collegiate Schools of Business (AACSB)–the International Association for Management Education recently initiated the first industry-wide management education assessment tool to capture faculty opinions, perceptions, and attitudes (American Assembly/Educational Benchmarking, 1998). The AACSB/EBI Management Education Faculty Study is a systematic and comprehensive analysis that compares faculty perceptions with a peer group of schools and the management education industry as a whole. Schools that choose to participate in the study pay an annual fee and receive questionnaires that are administered to the faculty.

The confidentiality of individual faculty who respond and the school as whole is achieved by following the administration policies of the well-planned survey. Tenured and nontenured faculty are separated into two distinct segments for analysis. At most schools, tenured and tenure-track faculty represent the vast majority of faculty included in the survey and are the groups most involved in the success of the school. Once the questionnaire is administered to the faculty and returned to AACSB/EBI, the school is asked to choose a set of institutions with which to conduct a comparative analysis (called in the analysis the "Select 6"). The results are then returned to the participating schools for review by the dean and faculty and use as part of an overall continuous improvement program. The survey measures faculty perceptions of the level of support for faculty development in teaching skills, research skills and funded research, computer technology, addressing global issues, and multidisciplinary research/teaching. The survey also gathers information about tenure/posttenure and annual review processes, salary, faculty workload, school leadership, teaching effectiveness, overall faculty satisfaction, and many other areas. The results of participation in the first year of the AACSB/EBI study in 1998 by the Hagan School of Business at Iona College are shown in Figure 7. This institution is an example of a typical private independent college that is tuition driven. A separate demographic profile of survey respondents found that of all tenured faculty in the business school at Iona College, 81% responded to the survey and that they averaged 22 years of experience as a faculty member.

The survey had a total of 88 questions, categorized into the 15 areas shown on Figure 7. According to the results, business faculty surveyed about faculty development (section 2 in the survey) perceived they had a strong sense of support, and Iona College was ranked first when compared with the six peer schools. Other areas where faculty reported positive perceptions included tenure/posttenure and annual review processes, support in service projects, technical support for computer hardware and software applications, business school administration/leadership, faculty influence, teaching effectiveness, the school's culture, and overall satisfaction. This type of assessment of the faculty's perceptions is useful for evaluating posttenure faculty

FIGURE 7

Sample Results from the 1998 AACSB/EBI Management Education Faculty Survey: Satisfaction of Tenured and Tenure Track Faculty at Iona College

	Your School		Select 6 Comparative Analysis			
	Mean score	*Rank among 7 schools*	*Mean score*	*Mini-mum score*	*Maxi-mum score*	*
1. Level of support faculty receive						
—Research assistants/grants	3.26	5	3.28	2.52	3.98	
—Teaching assistants/grants	3.31	5	3.26	2.54	4.14	
—Service: university/school/ professional	5.02	1	3.91	2.78	4.49	▲
—Travel/international activities/ sabbaticals/secretarial aid	4.79	4	4.36	2.82	4.96	
—Computer hardware/software	5.70	2	4.93	3.15	5.94	▲
2. Level of support for faculty development						
—Teaching skills and new pedagogy	5.27	1	4.07	2.77	5.22	▲
—Research skills and funded research	4.57	1	3.38	2.47	4.10	▲
—Computer technology	5.56	1	4.33	2.90	5.31	▲
—Addressing global issues	5.48	1	4.36	3.36	5.15	▲
—Multidisciplinary research/ teaching	5.11	1	3.88	2.85	4.44	▲
3. Faculty compensation/promotion						
—Salary	3.19	5	3.73	2.33	4.44	
—Tenure, posttenure, and annual review processes	3.98	2	3.67	2.39	4.31	▲
4. Faculty teaching workload						
—Teaching load	3.73	6	4.23	3.11	4.82	▼
—Class size/classroom facilities	5.02	1	4.37	3.62	4.79	▲
—Student evaluations	4.26	2	3.61	3.17	4.29	▲
5. Business school administration/ leadership						
—Articulation of vision and goals	5.77	1	4.28	2.51	5.33	▲
—Academic freedom/will of faculty	4.69	3	4.23	2.66	5.20	
—Allocation of resources	5.22	1	3.75	2.41	5.02	▲
—Quality of appointments	4.95	2	4.57	3.57	5.05	▲
—External: Resource acquisition/ relationships	4.20	2	3.43	2.37	4.22	
—Teaching assignments/ schedules	5.21	3	4.88	4.21	5.54	
—Negotiating for departmental resources	4.75	1	3.96	2.76	4.62	▲

FIGURE 7

Sample Results From the 1998 AACSB/EBI Management Education Faculty Survey: Satisfaction of Tenured and Tenure Track Faculty at Iona College *(Continued)*

6. Ability of faculty to influence:						▲
—Tenure/promotion decisions	4.63	2	4.21	2.89	5.12	▲
—Policy/curriculum development	4.68	2	4.35	3.40	4.82	▲
—Resource allocations	4.05	2	3.51	2.46	4.38	
7. External consulting practices	4.30	4	4.30	3.67	5.20	▲
8. Faculty teaching effectiveness	5.09	1	4.64	3.97	5.04	▲
9. Program evaluation: MBA	5.28	2	4.67	4.10	5.29	▲
10. Program evaluation: Undergraduate	5.01	3	4.77	4.10	5.10	
11. Program evaluation: Doctoral	NA	NA	4.32	4.32	4.32	
12. Placement	4.00	4	4.25	3.29	5.29	
13. Culture						
—Shared common vision	5.17	1	3.64	2.19	4.17	▲
—Quality of relationship/ mentoring/collegiality	5.59	1	4.18	3.05	4.78	▲
14. Colleagues	3.96	7	4.64	3.99	5.96	▼
15. The bottom line: Overall satisfaction	5.93	1	5.34	4.24	5.93	▲

▲ = Select 6 rank: 1 or 2 = ▲; 3, 4, or 5 = blank; 6 or 7 = ▼
NA: Not applicable.
Source: American Assembly/Educational Benchmarking, 1998, p. 3. Used with permission.

development activities and overall faculty management practices in a school or department. EBI plans to adapt the Management Education Faculty Survey for use with faculty from other disciplines, including art and sciences, engineering, and teacher education. (For more information about EBI, see Appendix A.)

Deans and faculty development directors can also use more objective assessment measures, including annual data on the scholarly productivity and service activities of tenured faculty, student evaluations, grant funds received, use of active learning strategies, use of instructional technology, teaching load, total instructional credit hours, and so on. There are many ways to gather and measure these data using charts and tables, and some institutions link these outcome measurements directly with their strategic plans using campus-wide information systems. They then use these results as a basis for individual, program, and departmental budget funding allocations. This kind of linkage between the mission-based strategic plan (which may include developing tenured faculty) and the outcomes achieved can be a most effective method for ensuring the leadership's full implementation of the institution's goals.

Options for Nondeveloping Tenured Faculty

Even if the leadership and most faculty of the institution fully support posttenure faculty development and it is effectively implemented and assessed, some tenured faculty may not continue to develop and improve. They are usually a very small number of the faculty at most institutions, but they can damage development efforts for other faculty. For those individuals, and to help ensure the effective development of other tenured faculty who want to continue to grow and learn, the institution should consider other alternatives, such as termination proceedings or an early retirement policy. In the case of termination, proper due process should be followed. Those institutions with a formal posttenure review process already have the mechanism in place to accomplish the proper "weeding" or termination of faculty who are not growing. Optional early retirement or phased retirement is another option (Broder, 1997; Ohio University, 1997). Such policies often include retirement incentives and phased retirement programs that serve the interests of the institution in continuous renewal of its human resources. This program provides opportunities to respond to changes in program and staffing needs and thus create more options for institutional development. Although the institution will consider individual faculty member's personal and professional needs in extending the privilege of the retirement incentive or phased retirement programs, the policies are intended to facilitate actual retirement.

For example, the policy at American University offers individuals who have served the university as a full-time member of the teaching faculty for 20 years, excluding leaves without pay, the opportunity to apply for the retirement incentive program, provided his or her age plus years of service (20 or more) equals or is greater than 80 (Broder, 1997; Ohio University, 1997). The university may limit the policy for certain individuals, depending on the needs of the institution and the academic department in which the faculty member serves. Faculty members electing the retirement incentive program who meet the age and service criteria receive payments according to a set schedule and other benefits, including some health coverage. A phased retirement program is slightly different, involving a reduced teaching, service, and research load for a reduced salary and better benefits. These programs, in conjunction with a formal posttenure review system (and a development component) can motivate senior faculty to increase their performance and continue to develop or to leave the institution. If the college or university does not have a formal posttenure review system but has other optional development programs, the early retirement programs can also be useful, particularly if the administration informs senior faculty that expectations are increased and that they will experience stronger consequences for nonperformance and nondevelopment. These consequences can involve teaching load, teaching schedule, travel support, office location, departmental structure, technology support, and other factors that may help certain faculty make their decision to develop or to retire. Posttenure faculty development does not need to come to this for all faculty, but for some individuals it may be necessary.

A very informative publication for assistance in developing senior tenured faculty is *A Handbook for New Practitioners* (Wadsworth, 1988). It is a good reference for administrators and faculty who want to learn more about how to establish and improve development programs for faculty at all stages of their careers. It is important to properly staff posttenure faculty programs with developers who have good communication skills, can build a support network that encourages collegiality and an intellectual environment, and will encourage positive performance improvements by tenured faculty. The faculty's acceptance can be obtained by getting faculty involved early in the development of the program, and it should be maintained through mechanisms such as a faculty advisory board or committee and involve department chairs. In addition to a strong sense of faculty ownership, development programs for tenured faculty should be supported strongly but

It is important to properly staff posttenure faculty programs with developers who have good communication skills.

discreetly by the administration, which can also support and guide outcomes assessment for continuous improvement.

A significant amount of useful advice is available on how to create a system of faculty development that helps faculty improve and feel appreciated. It is important for institutions to learn from the successes of other colleges and universities and build programs that fit the mission and academic culture in which their faculty are working.

CONCLUSION

The external environment increasingly influences higher education in many ways, as described in this monograph. As technology progresses in this digital age and we continue to move from a postindustrial to an information society, organizations such as colleges and universities must make an extra effort to keep their employees up to date and continually learning. There is no sustainable competitive advantage today other than organizational learning (Senge, 1990; Tapscott, 1996). Organizations can compete only if they can learn faster than the opposition and overcome any organizational learning disabilities. New educational competition from institutions such as The National Technological University and the University of Phoenix is forcing traditional colleges and universities to change the way things traditionally have been done. And the competition is doing so with new arrangements for faculty employment and by using new technology to reach out to students with educational programs that are current, innovative, and cost less than traditional programs. Moreover, other external factors influence traditional institutions: changing student and faculty demographics, support levels from government bodies, accreditation requirements, and an overall change in the public's perception of the tenure system.

As discussed in the first section, some observers view tenure as one of the potential organizational learning disabilities that tradition-bound institutions must overcome or eliminate (Breneman, 1997; Chabotar and Honan, 1997). Others do not believe, however, that having tenure is at odds with continuous improvement and learning. Instead of elimination, one way to overcome this disability (while tenure is still in place) is through posttenure faculty development strategies. In fact, research has shown that older (tenured) faculty members are more likely to participate in faculty development programs than younger faculty (Mbuh, 1993). Similarly, faculty members with more years of experience are more likely to participate than those with fewer years of experience. The strategies reported in this monograph and proposed in the general model include creating optional development programs and making development plans part of a formal posttenure review process. After reading the literature, collecting information about processes and outcomes from colleges and universities, and reading various discussions about these issues, the author of this report believes that the best method for most institutions is to not link posttenure faculty development programs directly with any formal posttenure review process. Posttenure review should have development as the primary goal, with a development plan that is triggered by nonperformance. The best approach is a comprehensive system of optional development opportunities with an annual development plan, combined with merit pay and strong administrative leadership to ensure that improvement activities reach all tenured faculty. Both those institutions with posttenure review processes and those without should offer effective posttenure development strategies based on the mission, needs, and size of the institution. Smaller colleges can offer development programs under the direction of a full-time tenured faculty member who is awarded release time. Larger institutions should create an office for faculty development with a full-time director and support staff. The faculty development mission statement in all types of institutions should address the needs of both new and tenured faculty. Research has shown that needs vary by type of institution in posttenure review policy purposes, processes, and components, including faculty development (Harris, 1996).

A review of the literature on faculty development clearly indicates that the emphasis should be on institutional strategies that go beyond one-shot solutions and quick cures (Clark and others, 1990). A rational institutional approach to addressing concerns about posttenure faculty development would be to first determine what the needs are, then develop systematic and comprehensive solutions that motivate the faculty to take part. In a recent discussion about posttenure faculty development on the Higher Education Process Faculty Development electronic mail listserv (Wise, 1995), a professor of business explained that to motivate people to want a product or service, three things must occur: (a) the people must be aware of their needs; (b) the people must be aware of the product and service and what it can do or not do; and (c) the people must perceive that a match exists between the service and meeting those needs. These items are part of the rationale behind getting tenured faculty involved in designing faculty development programs, serving on advisory boards for faculty development centers, and serving as program directors. Programs designed by tenured faculty may be less likely to be quick, one-shot attempts at solving specific problems and may help address the issue of posttenure faculty development more broadly. Examples include career change programs (Clark and others, 1990), growth contracting (Smith, 1976), faculty development plans, and other faculty development initiatives. In addition, other research has shown that a faculty development program that is faculty owned and institutionally supported can alleviate problems of morale and inertia among faculty (Panfor, 1996).

For members of the tenured faculty majority, who are threatened with this stagnation as colleges and universities become more "tenured in," professional development must bring renewal (Lindquist, 1981). Faculty development is essentially a form of adult development, and tenured faculty members need to be made aware that everyone progresses through stages in his or her personal and professional lives. Programs for tenured faculty should involve personal development strategies to address this need. Part of the reason for the morale problem may concern how the faculty and administration view teaching at the institution—as a craft, a profession, art, or labor (Harris, Bennett, and Preedy, 1997). Teaching, along with the other main elements of being a faculty member (research and service), is probably a combination of all four views of work. Some tenured faculty today find that designing new courses, writing journal articles, and serving with their colleagues is truly rewarding and brings them renewal. Others, however, could use some assistance from the institution in bringing them into the "fold" and reengaging them with the benefits and joys of college faculty life. This monograph has reported several examples of effective strategies whose results include perceptible improvement in faculty members' motivation and productivity. Nevertheless, reasonable efforts at bringing renewal will not be successful for some faculty. For those faculty, options for termination unfortunately must sometimes be used.

The future of faculty development and posttenure strategies will continue to evolve as the new technologies and competition transform basic college teaching processes (Graf and others, 1992). The methods of teaching, research, and service, as well as the content of the curriculum, will change to meet the needs of the marketplace. American colleges and universities are poised at the edge of a remarkable transformation at the same time an unprecedented though silent demographic change in the profile of the faculty is occurring (Finkelstein, Seal, and Schuster, 1998). Institutions with effective posttenure faculty development systems will be better able to compete and thrive than those that do not help develop their tenured faculty.

APPENDIX A: Resources for Faculty Development

- The Professional and Organizational Development Network in Higher Education is a professional association of people who share a commitment to improving higher education. Members are typically engaged in faculty, administrative, instructional, or organizational development activities. The network helps its members find resources for renewal, explore common interests and concerns, exchange information and ideas, and enhance professional skills through an annual conference, the annual book of readings, *To Improve the Academy,* a newsletter, a membership directory, regional meetings, and a summer institute that provides training in professional development issues. For more information: *http://www.public.iastate.edu/~POD_Network*

- POD-L mailing list, operated by the Professional and Organizational Development Network in Higher Education. This e-mail discussion list is a way for members of POD to continue interaction between conferences and newsletters as they work in faculty, instructional, and organizational development supporting teaching in higher education. Uses of the list include communicating ideas, reflections, successes, cautions, or news. Also of interest is the ability to seek references or information from previous discussions that are stored in the archive. For more information: *pod-request@iastate.edu*

- TIAA-CREF created the Hesburgh Award to acknowledge and reward successful, innovative faculty development programs that enhance undergraduate teaching and help inspire the growth of such initiatives at America's colleges and universities. For information about the winners each year: *http://www.tiaa-cref.org:80./siteline/set-hesburgh.html*

Additional information about announcements and entry procedures can be obtained from:

Teachers Insurance and Annuity Association/College Retirement Equities Fund
601 Thirteenth Street, NW, Suite 1100-N
Washington, DC 20005.

- EBI. In administering faculty development activities, including posttenure strategies, it can be useful to measure how the faculty being served perceive the processes. It is also useful to discover how the perceptions at one institution compare with perceptions at similar or competitive colleges and universities. Educational Benchmarking Inc., in cooperation with the American Assembly of Colleges and Schools of Business–The International Association for Management Education, recently began an annual survey of management education faculty. Seventy-one business schools participated in the inaugural year of the project, which will be offered by AACSB/EBI each spring for the next several years. The comprehensive survey addresses faculty attitudes and perceptions in many areas, including *faculty support* through research assistance, teaching assistance, and grants; *faculty development* of teaching skill, research skills, and use of technology; *faculty compensation and promotion* in terms of satisfaction with salary level, the promotion/tenure system, and posttenure processes; *faculty teaching/workload* in terms of satisfaction with teaching load, class size, and teaching evaluation processes; and *faculty influence* regarding promotion and tenure decisions, policy development, and allocation of resources.

The analysis is presented by academic discipline, academic rank, tenure status, and demographics, and for the entire faculty. Participating schools may request an analysis of their faculty alone or a comparison with six other programs chosen. The cost of participation in 1998 was $895. EBI plans to offer faculty survey projects for other disciplines, including arts and sciences, engineering, and teacher education. For more information, contact:

Educational Benchmarking Inc.
215 Jefferson Road
St. Louis, MO 63119
Telephone: 314-963-1018
E-mail: *Ebiebi@asl.com*
ARNOLD© is a database of faculty, administrators, and staff in higher education around the world who have

registered with the database because they have one or more of the following interests:

- *Exchange*—Individuals seeking opportunities for teaching, research, or administration in new settings. These individuals seek partners with similar backgrounds, credentials, and interests to effect a reciprocal and temporary exchange of employment sites. Individuals may also be seeking temporary or visiting situations that would allow for short-term positions at other sites while maintaining their employment status at their home institutions.
- *Collaboration*—Individuals who are interested in finding partners for collaboration in instructional and research projects.
- *Position search*—Individuals seeking a permanent change in their employment status.

ARNOLD© is also a database of temporary and permanent position openings at colleges and universities around the world. It is designed with a series of multiple delimiting features to help users define and limit their search to those individuals and/or situations that will meet their needs. The user can contact individuals and/or situations of interest through e-mail, snail mail, telephone, or facsimile. Exploration of possibilities and potential is up to the user and those who are contacted. The two parties involved are responsible for finalizing arrangements for exchange, collaboration, or employment. To register, individuals may go directly to the Registration Form and supply the requested information at *http://arnold.snybuf.edu/html/DATABASE_ MENU.HTML.* Institutions need a user code to post positions, which can be requested from ARNOLD© electronically or by e-mailing *wicklawb @buffalostate.edu.*

ARNOLD© is supported through modest institutional user fees; the cost of unlimited postings for institutions is $100 for 6 months.

- HEPROC is a well-developed, well-maintained community of thoughtful educators who serve each other as networking partners. Comprising 2,200 members in 40 countries and more than a dozen forums covering specialized subjects, HEPROC can help with research and informational needs. Individuals can (a) explore forum topics, (b) subscribe to forums, (c) send a research question to the forum of their choice, and (d) read HEPROC's Core Values.

HEPROC was begun in October 1993 with a listserv-based forum that employed innovative segmentation to facilitate dialogue. In summer 1994, a Web service was added. The moderator tends to keep HEPROC focused on forum discussions using e-mail, and the HEPROC Web site is a way to help people find the forums. Over time, HEPROC has offered different services. A trademark of R&R Publishers, Inc., HEPROC offers 13 forums covering a wide range of topics, including creation of faculty development workshops; attendance at faculty development workshops; collective bargaining and salary rationalization; compensation models that enable and encourage shared benefits (and risk taking) between faculty and the institution; training for curriculum changes; support for faculty development; support for faculty members' private efforts at development; faculty compensation; tenure issues; development of senior faculty; faculty apathy; merit pay; and input from students about faculty compensation and training. For more information, *http://heproc.org*

- The Center for Educational Development and Assessment (CEDA) is a private consulting corporation founded for the purpose of translating research in the field of evaluation and assessment into operational practices and programs. CEDA has been offering consulting services and professional enrichment seminars and workshops for college and university faculty and administrators since 1988. These workshops and seminars focus on designing, developing, and operating faculty evaluation systems and instructional development programs, as well as assessing and developing academic leadership skills. Thousands of professionals from more than 350 colleges and universities of all sizes and types have attended CEDA workshops. Past participants include faculty, faculty senate presidents, faculty union leaders, directors, department chairs, deans, vice presidents, presidents, and system chancellors. CEDA's goals are to (a) assist academic leaders in developing and implementing valid, reliable faculty evaluation systems; and (b) provide professional enrichment resources to assist faculty in their continuing efforts to enhance their instructional design, development, and assessment skills.

For more information and to see current workshop offerings, contact:

Center for Educational Development and Assessment
P. O. Box 172314
Memphis, TN 38187-2314
Telephone: 901-758-1627
E-mail: *cedanet@aol.com*
Web site: *http://members.aol.com/cedanet/ceda.html*

APPENDIX B: NUPROF Program at the University of Nebraska–Lincoln

Office of Professional and Organizational Development
Institute of Agricultural and Natural Resources

Purpose

Faculty are constantly required to be in a continual state of personal and professional change. NUPROF provides an avenue for personal and professional assessment directed toward professional renewal.

Program

NUPROF allows participants to examine the path of their careers in the context of the needs of IANR and to plan a sequence of activities to guide their professional growth. The program includes:

- *Entry.* Faculty members indicate their desire to participate, attend an informational meeting, confer with department heads or unit administrators, submit an application, and, contingent upon approval from the appropriate dean, are admitted to the program.
- *Faculty Development Institute.* To initiate the process, participants attend a 3-day retreat off campus. The purpose is to gain a better understanding of oneself and the nature of change, to initiate a search for alternatives, and to learn some methods for career planning. Because the Faculty Development Institute is an integral part of NUPROF, participants are asked to clear their calendars so they can attend.
- *Exploring options and gathering information.* Over a period of weeks or months, each participant investigates professional, career, teaching, research, and extension alternatives; confers with resource persons, peers, appropriate administrators, and family members; and identifies personal and professional needs as well as those of the unit, discipline, and clientele. Participants work in self-directed trios or small groups during this phase.
- *Growth plans.* After attending a work session on writing growth plans, each participant can submit a growth plan to the campus steering committee for funding. Growth plans may take into account long-range as well as immediate objectives. Funded for up to $1,500, growth

plans represent a commitment to a statement of goals, outcomes, and proposed activity.

- *Implementation.* Participants carry out growth plans in time periods ranging from a few months to a year. NUPROF growth plans may be the first step in longer range plans for additional study (e.g., faculty development leaves) or other career development activities.
- *Evaluation.* Approximately 12 to 18 months after entering the program, each participant evaluates the achievement of his or her growth plans and defines the next steps.

Avenues for Growth

The heart of NUPROF is the professional renewal and development of its participants. Growth plans, the stated individual project proposals indicating what action the faculty member expects to implement, may fall into any of the following areas:

- *Subject matter.* Updates and new knowledge in the discipline, interdisciplinary study, new discipline development;
- *Methodology.* Problem solving in a discipline, laboratory learning, computer-aided instruction, distance learning, adult learners, alternate delivery systems, integration of values and ethics, integration of the international perspective, improving communication skills;
- *New technologies.* Computer hardware and software, robotics, microsurgery, microprocessors, electronic engineering, biotechnology;
- *Human relations.* Creative problem solving, team building, interpersonal communications, management, leadership.

How to Enter NUPROF

A new class of NUPROF is formed each fall. Orientation sessions are held in late August. After these sessions, faculty can decide to apply to enter the program. After acceptance into the program, all participants are expected to attend the Faculty Development Institute, a 3-day personal assessment experience in the fall. Upon return from the Faculty Development Institute, faculty begin a process of exploration to decide an area for which to write a growth plan.

Faculty are ineligible for NUPROF if they

1. Do not currently have tenure (applies to teaching and research);
2. Have not been with the university for more than 6 years (extension);
3. Do not have faculty status.

What Can NUPROF Provide?

- Coordination of individual and organizational needs
- Structure for planned change and to address changing institutional priorities
- Collegiality across department and disciplines
- A group committed to professional growth
- Resource people to address various issues involving career and growth
- Some financial resources (seed money)
- Networking possibilities (both ideas and financial resources)
- Opportunities for redirection (different roles as well as new professional dimensions)

NUPROF Outcomes

- Reflective career/life planning
- Coordination of individual and institutional needs
- Creation of a norm of risk taking
- Growth plan providing a temporary structure during a time of change
- An institutional structure for planned change
- Encouragement of "negotiations" between the faculty member and the unit administrator
- Collegiality across departments and divisions
- Often, faculty development leaves (sabbaticals)
- A range of changes, from learning new methods or techniques to changes in professional roles to a career shift (Office of Professional and Organizational Development 1997a, pp. 1–2)

APPENDIX C: Sample Guidelines for a Faculty Development Plan

Hagan School of Business, Iona College
Guidelines for Completing the Faculty Development Plan

As discretionary budget support (e.g., travel) will be based on this year's Faculty Development Plan, please return your completed plan to your department chair (with a copy to the dean) by early September.

The first step is getting closure on your previous year's plan by identifying your accomplishments and areas for improvement. Next, consider the following guidelines to assist your thorough completion of this year's plan:

I. Teaching and Student Learning
This is a critical focus for the Hagan School and therefore is listed first. What are your goals for improving your teaching and encouraging student learning for this year? In answering this question, consider the following:

- What are you doing to remain current in your teaching field(s)?
- List the course/curriculum development projects you are currently working on, along with anticipated completion dates.
- How do you know that students are learning in your courses? What evidence of learning outcomes exists beyond examinations?
- Are you requiring students to work in teams as active participants in the class?
- How have you improved your syllabus since the last time that you taught the course?
- Are you covering ethics, international business, diversity, and technology as well as integrating computing and library/writing projects in your courses?

II. Intellectual Contributions and Professional Development
Our excellence as teachers—as facilitators of student learning—requires that we remain active learners ourselves. What are your goals this year for making intellectual contributions and continuing professional development? The traditional benchmark is journal publications, which we encourage, especially in the applied and pedagogical areas. Our Faculty Development Research Initiative is aimed

specifically at publications—converting our presentations, proceedings, and working papers into publishable form. At the same time, we want a portfolio of contributions indicative of overall high quality. We therefore encourage and recognize broadly diverse contributions and development activities. Here are some thoughts to consider in this area:

- List the research and scholarly writing projects you are currently working on, along with anticipated completion dates.
- What are your current areas of research interest?
- How are your intellectual contributions and professional development activities related to the courses that you teach?
- What is your emphasis for contributions—applied, instructional/pedagogical, or basic (theoretical)?
- List some "hot" issues in your field and how these issues are affecting your research and teaching activities.
- List all the professional development projects that you are currently engaged in (e.g., training seminars, conferences, continuing education) and those that you expect to pursue during this year.

III. Service

Service is a major part of our mission as a college. The service area is broad and includes department-, school-, and college-wide activities, the business and professional community, and the community at large. What are your goals this year for the service area? Here are some thoughts:

- How are you involved in student advisement (e.g., first-year students, departmental majors, career counseling)?
- What other services will you provide to our students to meet their needs?
- What school and college committees will you serve on?
- Are you contributing professional services pro bono?
- What community activities are you involved in?

REFERENCES

Aleamoni, L. M. (1990). Faculty development research in colleges, universities, and professional schools: The challenge. *Journal of Personnel Evaluation in Education, 3*(2), 193–195.

Alstete, J. W. (1995). *Benchmarking in higher education: Adapting best practices to improve quality.* ASHE-ERIC Higher Education Report (Vol. 24, No. 5). Washington, DC: George Washington University, Graduate School of Education and Human Development.

Alstete, J. W. (1997). The correlates of administrative decentralization. *Journal of Education for Business, 73*(1), 21–28.

Alstete, J. W. (1999). *Hagan School of Business faculty course evaluation report: Fall 1998 semester and trimester* [Internal report]. New Rochelle, NY: Iona College.

Altman, H. B. (1986). *Building faculty support for faculty development at research universities.* Paper presented at Faculty Evaluation and Development: Lessons Learned, Kansas City, MO.

American Association of University Professors. (1997). *Standards for good practice in post-tenure review* [On-line], 1–13. Available: www.igc.apc.org/aaup/postten.htm

American Assembly of Collegiate Schools of Business. (1994). New benchmarking survey makes business schools introspective. *Newsline, 25*(1), 16–17.

American Assembly of Collegiate Schools of Business/Educational Benchmarking Inc. (1998). *1998 AACSB/EBI management education faculty survey results.* St. Louis, MO: Author.

Andrews, H. A. (1987). *Merit in education: Assessing merit pay as the catalyst to pay and evaluation reforms.* Stillwater, OK: New Forums Press.

Argyris, C., and Schön, D. A. (1978). *Organizational learning: A theory of action perspective.* Reading, MA: Addison-Wesley.

ARNOLD©. (1997, March 27). *Academic resource network on-line database.* Buffalo State College and the Research Foundation of the State University of New York. Retrieved July 8, 1998, from ARNOLD: http://arnold.snybuff.edu

Atkins, S. S., Hagseth, J. A., and Arnold, E. L. (1990). The faculty developer as witch doctor: Envisioning and creating the future. *To Improve the Academy, 9,* 83–88.

Austin, A. E., Brocato, J. J., and Rohrer, J. D. (1997). Institutional missions: Implications for faculty development. *To Improve the Academy, 16,* 3–20.

Baez, B., and Centra, J. A. (1995). *Tenure, promotion, and reappointment: Legal and administrative implications.*

ASHE-ERIC Higher Education Report (Vol. 24, No. 1). Washington, DC: George Washington University, Graduate School of Education and Human Development.

Baldridge, J. V., Curtis, D. V., Ecker, G., and Riley, G. L. (1978). *Policy making and effective leadership.* San Francisco: Jossey-Bass.

Bennett, J. B., and Chater, S. S. (1984). Evaluating the performance of tenured faculty members. *Educational Record, 65*(2), 38–41.

Bergquist, W. H., and Phillips, S. R. (1975). Components of an effective faculty development program. *Journal of Higher Education, 46,* 177–211.

Bergquist, W. H., and Phillips, S. R. (1977). *Handbook for faculty development* (Vol. 2). Council for the Advancement of Small Colleges in association with the College Center of the Finger Lakes.

Bernstein, G. (1986). *Five years of an effective faculty development program.* Paper presented at Faculty Evaluation and Development: Lessons Learned, Kansas City, MO.

Blackburn, R. T., Pellino, A., Boberg, A., and O'Connell, W. R. (1980). Faculty development programs, the improvement of instruction, and faculty goals: An evaluation. *Current Issues in Higher Education, 1*(2), 32–48.

Bland, C. J., and Bergquist, W. H. (1997). *The vitality of senior faculty members: Snow on the roof—fire in the furnace.* ASHE-ERIC Higher Education Report (Vol. 25, No. 7). Washington, DC: George Washington University, Graduate School of Education and Human Development.

Bland, C. J., and Schmitz, C. C. (1988). Faculty vitality on review. *Journal of Higher Education, 59*(2), 190–224.

Blum, D. E. (1989, October 18). Concept of merit pay for professors spreads as competition among institutions grows. *Chronicle of Higher Education,* A1.

Boice, R. (1992). *The new faculty member: Supporting and fostering professional development.* San Francisco: Jossey-Bass.

Bowen, H. R., and Schuster, J. H. (1986). *American professors: A national resource imperiled.* New York: Oxford University Press.

Bowman, M. A. (1991). *Administrative and faculty development: A study of academic chairpersons.* Kalamazoo, MI: Western Michigan University.

Boyer, E. L. (1990). *Scholarship reconsidered: Priorities of the professoriate.* Princeton, NJ: Carnegie Foundation for the Advancement of Teaching.

Braskamp, L. A., and Ory, J. C. (1994). *Assessing Faculty Work.* San Francisco: Jossey-Bass.

Breneman, D. W. (1997). *Alternatives to tenure for the next generation of academics* (Working Paper Series Inquiry No. 14). Washington, DC: American Association for Higher Education.

Brittain, A. W. (1992, July 22). Pitfalls in evaluating tenured faculty. *Chronicle of Higher Education,* B3.

Broder, I. (1997). *The university retirement program* [Memo]. Washington, DC: American University. Retrieved July 14, 1998, from the World Wide Web: http://www.american.edu/academic.depts/provost/retire.htm

Centra, J. A. (1976). *Faculty development practices in U. S. colleges and universities* (Project Report 76–30). Princeton, NJ: Educational Testing Service.

Centra, J. A. (1978). Types of faculty development programs. *Journal of Higher Education, 49*(2), 151–162.

Centra, J. A. (1985). Maintaining faculty vitality through faculty development. In S. M. Clark and D. R. Lewis (Eds.), *Faculty vitality and institutional productivity* (pp. 141–156). New York: Columbia University, Teachers College.

Chabotar, K. J., and Honan, J. P. (1997). *New yardsticks to measure financial distress* (Working Paper Series Inquiry No. 4). Washington, DC: American Association for Higher Education.

Chait, R., and Trower, C. A. (1997). *Where tenure does not reign: Colleges with contract systems* (Working Paper Series Inquiry1 No. 3). Washington, DC: American Association for Higher Education.

Chandler, J. B. (1988). Faculty renewal: Balancing personal and professional life. An individual responsibility, an institutional commitment. In E. C. Wadsworth (Ed.), *A handbook for new practitioners* (pp. 133–137). Stillwater, OK: New Forums Press.

Chesky, J. (1997). *My experiences PTR* [On-line]. Available: ptr@listserv.temple.edu

Clark, S. M., and Corcoran, M. E. (1989, Fall). Faculty renewal and change. *New Directions for Institutional Research, 63,* 19–32.

Clark, S. M., Corcoran, M. E., and Lewis, D. R. (1990). The case for an institutional perspective on faculty development. In M. J. Finkelstein (Ed.), *ASHE Reader on Faculty and Faculty Issues* (2nd ed., pp. 308–323). Needham Heights, MA: Ginn Press.

College of Charleston. (1996, August). *Information for faculty research and development support: The faculty research and development committee.* Retrieved July 6, 1998, from the World Wide Web: http://www.cofc.edu/academic/faculty/research.html

Cox, M. D. (1998, February 6). *Faculty development centers: Engaging faculty for performance improvement.* Paper presented at the AACSB Undergraduate Program Seminar, Charlottesville, VA.

Cramer, O. (1997). *Re: PTR and Colleges.* Available: ptr@listserv. temple.edu.

Crawley, A. L. (1995). Senior faculty renewal at research universities: Implications for academic policy development. *Innovative Higher Education, 20*(2), 71–94.

Davies, P. (Ed.). (1981). *The American heritage dictionary of the English language* (3rd ed.). New York: Dell Publishing.

Diamond, R. M. (1988). Faculty development, instructional development, and organizational development: Options and choices. In E. C. Wadsworth (Ed.), *A handbook for new practitioners* (pp. 9–11). Stillwater, OK: New Forums Press.

Diamond, R. M., and Adam, B. E. (1998). *Changing priorities at research universities, 1991–1996.* [Based on *The national study of research universities on the balance between research and undergraduate teaching,* 1992, ISBN-0-87411-960-X.] Syracuse, NY: Syracuse University, Center for Instructional Development.

Ditwiler, E. (1997). *Merit pay discussion.* HEPROC Institutional Development. Available: listserv@heproc.org

Eble, K. E., and McKeachie, W. J. (1985). *Improving undergraduate education through faculty development: An analysis of effective programs and practices.* San Francisco: Jossey-Bass.

Eble, K. E., and McKeachie, W. J. (1990). Evolution of faculty development efforts. In M. J. Finkelstein (Ed.), *ASHE reader on faculty and faculty issues* (2nd ed., pp. 295–307). Needham Heights, MA: Ginn Press.

Educational Resources Information Center Clearinghouse on Higher Education. (1997). *Professional development* (pp. 1–3). Available: www.gwu.edu/~eriche/library/profdev.html

Erickson, B. L. (1986). *Faculty development at four-year colleges and universities: Lessons learned.* Paper presented at Faculty Evaluation and Development: Lessons Learned, Kansas City, MO.

Erickson, G. R., and Erickson, B. L. (1979). Improving college teaching: An evaluation of a teaching consultation procedure. *Journal of Higher Education, 50,* 670–683.

Erikson, E. (1977). *Childhood and society.* London: Triad/Granada.

Evergreen State College. (1996, May 14). *The Washington center for improving the quality of undergraduate education.* Retrieved February 21, 1999: http://192.211.16.13/katlinks/washcntr/home.html

Farber, B. A. (1983). A critical perspective on burnout. In B. A. Farber (Ed.), *Stress and burnout in the human service professions.* New York: Pergamon Press.

Farmer, D. W. (1993, Fall). Designing a reward system to promote career development in senior faculty. *New Directions for Teaching and Learning, 55,* 43–53.

Farr, G. (1988). Faculty development centers as resource centers. In E. C. Wadsworth (Ed.), *A handbook for new practitioners* (pp. 35–37). Stillwater, OK: New Forums Press.

Felicetti, D. A. (1989). Post-tenure review as a termination mechanism. *Journal for Higher Education Management, 4*(2), 51–55.

Finkelstein, M. J. (Ed.). (1990). *ASHE reader on faculty and faculty issues in colleges and universities* (2nd ed.). Needham Heights, MA: Ginn Press.

Finkelstein, M. J. (1993, Fall). The senior faculty: A portrait and literature review. *New Directions for Teaching and Learning, 55,* 7–19.

Finkelstein, M. J., and Jemmott, N. D. (1993, Fall). The senior faculty: Higher education's plentiful yet largely untapped resource. *New Directions for Teaching and Learning, 55,* 95–98.

Finkelstein, M. J., Seal, R. K., and Schuster, J. H. (1998). *The new academic generation: A profession in transformation.* Baltimore: Johns Hopkins University Press.

Francis, J. B. (1975). *How do we get there from here?* San Francisco: Jossey-Bass.

Frank, R. H., and Cook, P. J. (1995). *The winner-take-all society.* New York: Penguin.

Freedman, M. (Ed.). (1973). *Facilitating faculty development* (Vol. 1). San Francisco: Jossey-Bass.

Gaff, J. G. (1975). *Toward faculty renewal.* San Francisco: Jossey-Bass.

Gaff, J. G. (Ed.). (1978). Institutional renewal through the improvement of teaching. *New Directions for Higher Education* (Vol. 24). San Francisco: Jossey-Bass.

Gaff, J. G., and Wilson, R. C. (1971). The teaching environment. *AAUP Bulletin, 57,* 475–493.

Geis, G. L. (1977). Evaluation: Definitions, problems, and strategies. In C. K. Knapper et al. (Eds.), *If teaching is important* [Canadian Association of University Teachers Monograph Series]. Published by: Clarke, Irwin.

Goodman, M. J. (1994). The review of tenured faculty at a research university: Outcomes and appraisals. *Review of Higher Education, 18*(1), 83–94.

Graf, D. L., Albright, M. J., and Wheeler, D. W. (1992, Fall). Faculty development's role in improving undergraduate education. *New Directions for Teaching and Learning, 51,* 101–109.

Group for Human Development in Higher Education. (1974). Faculty development in a time of retrenchment. *Change.*

Hammons, J. O., and Wallace, T. H. S. (1976, December). Sixteen ways to kill a college faculty development program. *Educational Technology,* 16–20.

Handy, C. (1990). *Inside organizations.* London: BBC Books.

Harris, A., Bennett, N., and Preedy, M. (Eds.). (1997). *Organizational effectiveness and improvement in education.* Philadelphia: Open University Press.

Harris, B. J. (1996). The relationship between and among policy variables, type of institution, and perceptions of academic administrators with regard to post-tenure review. Unpublished doctoral dissertation, West Virginia University.

Herzberg, F. (1966). *Work and the nature of man.* New York: Staple Press.

Horn, J. M. (1998). On the ineffectiveness and irrelevancy of tenure. *Academic Questions, 11*(1), 19–27.

Hoyt, D. P., and Howard, G. S. (1978). The evaluation of faculty development programs. *Research in Higher Education, 8,* 25–38.

Huber, G. P. (1991). Organizational learning: The contributing processes and the literature. *Organizational Science, 2*(1), 88–115.

Indiana University Purdue University Indianapolis. (1998, June 16). *The center for teaching and learning.* Retrieved July 6, 1998, from the World Wide Web: http://www.center.iupui.edu/

Jarvis, P. (1997). Learning practical knowledge. In L. Kydd, M. Crawford, and C. Riches (Eds.), *Professional development for educational management.* London: Open University Press.

Johnson, G. E. R. (1993). Post-tenure review: Practical considerations. *Journal for Higher Education Management, 8*(2), 19–30.

Karpiak, I. E. (1997). University professors at mid-life: Being a part of . . . but feeling apart. *To Improve the Academy, 16,* 21–40.

Kelly, D. K. (1990). *Reviving the "deadwood": How to create an institutional climate to encourage the professional growth and revitalization of mid-career faculty in the community college* [Graduate Seminar Paper]. Claremont College.

Knefelkamp, L. L. (1990, May/June). Seasons of academic life: Honoring our collective autobiography. *Liberal Education, 76,* 4–11.

Koerin, B. B. (1980). Teaching effectiveness and faculty development programs: A review. *Journal of General Education, 32*(1), 40–51.

Kydd, L., Crawford, M., and Riches, C. (Eds.). (1997). *Professional development for educational management.* London: Open University Press.

Lang, H. G., and Conner, K. K. (1988). Some low-budget tips for faculty development programming. In E. C. Wadsworth (Ed.), *A Handbook for New Practitioners* (pp. 139–143). Stillwater, OK: New Forums Press.

Leatherman, C. (1998, June 26). AAUP offers guidance on post-tenure reviews. *Chronicle of Higher Education,* A13–A14.

Lee, J. (1995). *Tenure.* Washington, DC: National Education Association.

Leithwood, K. A. (1990). Lifeskills: Principals' role in teacher development. In B. M. Joyce (Ed.), *Changing school culture through staff development. 1990 yearbook of the Association for Supervision and Curriculum Development.* Alexandria, VA: ASCD.

Lewis, K. G., and Kristensen, E. (1997). A global faculty development network: The International Consortium for Educational Development (ICED). *To Improve the Academy, 16,* 53–66.

Licata, C. M. (1986). *Post-tenure faculty evaluation: Threat or opportunity?* ASHE-ERIC Higher Education Report No. 1. Washington, DC: Association for the Study of Higher Education.

Licata, C. M., and Morreale, J. C. (1997). Post-tenure review: Policies, practices, precautions, new pathways. In *Faculty careers and employment for the 21st century.* Washington, DC: American Association for Higher Education.

Lindquist, J. (1981). Professional development. In A. W. Chickering and Associates (Eds.), *The modern American college* (pp. 730–747). San Francisco: Jossey-Bass.

Lovelace, B. E., and LaBrecque, S. V. (1991). *A summary of reported policies and procedures of institutional plans for faculty development of postsecondary technical/vocational personnel.* Denton, TX: North Texas University, School of Human Resource Management.

Lucas, A. F. (1988). Maximizing impact on the organization: Teach chairs faculty development skills. In E. C. Wadsworth (Ed.), *A handbook for new practitioners* (pp. 157–161). Stillwater, OK: New Forums Press.

Luna, G., and Cullen, D. L. (1995). *Empowering the faculty: Mentoring redirected and renewed.* ASHE-ERIC Higher

Education Report (Vol. 24, No. 3). Washington, DC: George Washington University, Graduate School of Education and Human Development.

Lunde, J. P., and Healy, M. M. (1988). *Doing faculty development by committee*. Stillwater, OK: New Forums Press.

Magner, D. K. (1996, July 21). More colleges conduct post-tenure reviews. *Chronicle of Higher Education,* A13.

Martin, J. L., and Neal, A. D. (1997). How to stop the university from self-destructing. *Academic Questions, 10*(4), 46–50.

Maslow, A. (1970). *Motivation and personality*. New York: Harper and Row.

Mbuh, R. N. (1993). *Faculty perceptions of faculty development programs at the University of South Carolina: Implications for colleges and universities*. University of South Carolina.

McFerron, J. R., and others (1990, April). *A national study of the perception of administrative support for teaching and faculty development*. Paper presented at the annual meeting of the American Educational Research Association, Boston, MA.

McGregor, D. (1960). *The human side of enterprise*. New York: McGraw-Hill.

Metzger, W. P. (1955). *Academic freedom in the age of the university*. New York: Columbia University Press.

Meyer, H. H., Kay, E., and French, J. R. P., Jr. (1965). Split roles in performance appraisal. *Harvard Business Review, 43,* 123–129.

Miami University of Ohio. (1997). *Teaching grants, programs, resources, and events: 1997–98*. Oxford, OH: Author.

Moore, M. R. (1986, April). Post-tenure faculty development: Where is the adventure? *ACA Bulletin, 56,* 19–20.

Morreale, J. C., and Licata, C. M. (1997). *Post-tenure review: A guide book for academic administrators of colleges and schools of business*. St. Louis, MO: American Assembly of Collegiate Schools of Business.

Moscato, D. (1998). *Executive team meeting conversation*. New York: Iona College, Hagan School of Business.

National Center for Education Statistics. (1988). *National study of postsecondary faculty*. Washington, DC: U.S. Department of Education.

National Center for Education Statistics. (1993). *National study of postsecondary faculty*. Washington, DC: U.S. Department of Education. Retrieved January 1, 1999, from the World Wide Web: http://nces.ed.gov/

Neal, J. E. (1988). *Faculty evaluation: Its purposes and effectiveness*. Washington, DC: ERIC Clearinghouse on Higher Education.

Nelson, W. C. (1979). Faculty development: Prospects and potential for the 1980s. *Liberal Education, 65*(2), 141–149.

Nelson, W. C. (1981). *Renewal of the teacher scholar.* Washington, DC: Association of American Colleges.

Nelson, W. C., and Siegel, M. E. (1980). *Effective approaches to faculty development.* Washington, DC: Association of American Colleges.

New Jersey Institute for Collegiate Teaching and Learning. (1996, April 25). *NJICTL background.* Retrieved July 8, 1998, from the World Wide Web: http://www.shu.edu/programs/njictl/new/backgrd.html

Office of Professional and Organizational Development. (1997a, September 24). *NUPROF: A program for the professional renewal and redirection of faculty.* University of Nebraska–Lincoln, Institute of Agricultural and Natural Resources. Retrieved July 8, 1998, from the World Wide Web: http://ianrwww.unl.edu/opod/NUPROF.htm

Office of Professional and Organizational Development. (1997b, September 27). *An overview of OPOD.* University of Nebraska–Lincoln, Institute of Agriculture and Natural Resources. Retrieved July 8, 1998, from the World Wide Web: http://ianrwww.unl.edu/opod/overview.htm

Office of Professional and Organizational Development. (1997c, September 24). *A prospectus on faculty development leaves.* University of Nebraska–Lincoln, Institute of Agricultural and Natural Resources. Retrieved July 8, 1998, from the World Wide Web: http://ianrwww.unl.edu/opod/ leaves.htm

Ohio University. (1997, October 22). *Early retirement policy.* Retrieved July 14, 1998, from the World Wide Web: http://www.cats.ohiou.edu/~facsen/node71.html

Olswang, S. G., and Fantel, J. I. (1980). Tenure and periodic performance review: Compatible legal and administrative principles. *Journal of College and University Law, 7*(1–2), 1–30.

Panfor, S. C. (1996). *Needs assessment: An analysis of approaches for assessing the needs for a faculty development program at City Tech, City University of New York.* New York: Columbia University.

Partnership for College Teaching. (1996, April 25). *New Jersey Institute for Collegiate Teaching and Learning.* Retrieved July 8, 1998, from the World Wide Web: http://www.shu.edu/programs/njictl/new/pact~1.html

Parker, M. E. (1991). Faculty development: Essence of faculty and institutional vitality. *Journal of Dental Education, 55*(10), 656–658.

Perley, J. E. (1995). Tenure, academic freedom, and governance. *Academe, 81*(1), 43–47.

Postema, J. (1999). *Bush Foundation grants for faculty development.* Concordia College. Retrieved February 21, 1999, from the World Wide Web: http://www.cord.edu/dept/facultydev/bush.htm

Postle, D. (1989). *The mind gymnasium.* London: Macmillan.

Professional and Organizational Development Network in Higher Education. (1995, December 16). *Teaching Circles* [Listserv Discussion]. Retrieved July 12, 1998, from http://darkwing.uoregon.edu/~tep/library/articles/circles.html

Raufman, L. (1991). *Dimensions of faculty development: Organizational factors related to creating effective faculty programs in selected California community colleges.* University of California–Los Angeles.

Redditt, P. L., and Hamilton, W. T. (1978). Teaching improvement in a small college: Institutional renewal through the improvement of teaching. *New Directions for Higher Education* (Vol. 6). San Francisco: Jossey-Bass.

Reisman, B. (1986). Performance evaluation for tenured faculty: Issues and research. *Liberal Education, 72*(1), 73–87.

Rice, R. E. (1996). Making a place for the new American scholar. In *New pathways: Faculty careers and employment for the 21st century* (Vol. 1). Washington, DC: American Association for Higher Education.

Rifkin, T. (1995). *The status and scope of faculty evaluation* (ERIC Digest ED 385 315). Los Angeles: ERIC Clearinghouse for Community Colleges.

Rogers, C. (1967). *On becoming a person.* London: Constable.

Rubino, A. N. (1994). *Faculty development programs and evaluation in American colleges and universities.* Kalamazoo: Western Michigan University.

Rudolph, F. (1977). *Curriculum: A history of the American undergraduate course of study since 1636.* San Francisco: Jossey-Bass.

Schuster, J. H. (Ed.). (1990). *Enhancing faculty careers: Strategies for development and renewal.* San Francisco: Jossey-Bass.

Sell, G. R., and Chism, N. V. (1991). Finding the right match: Staffing faculty development centers. *To Improve the Academy, 10.*

Senge, P. M. (1990). *The fifth discipline: The art and practice of the learning organization.* New York: Doubleday.

Smith, A. B. (1976). *Faculty development and evaluation in higher education.* Washington, DC: ERIC Clearinghouse on Higher Education.

Smith, P. (1990). *Killing the spirit: Higher education in America.* New York: Penguin Books.

Sorcinelli, M. D. (1988). Encouraging excellence: Long-range planning for faculty development. In E. C. Wadsworth (Ed.), *A handbook for new practitioners* (pp. 27–34). Stillwater, OK: New Forums Press.

Southeast Missouri State University. (1996, November 20). *Merit Pay Guidelines. Faculty Senate.* Retrieved July 21, 1997, from http://economics.semo.edu/handbook/meritpay.htm

Stephen F. Austin State University. (1998, May 20). *What teaching circles are about at SFA.* Nacagdoches, Texas. Retrieved July 12, 1998, from http://hubel.sfasu.edu/otherendev/tc/teachcir.html

Stordahl, B. (1981, March). Faculty development: A survey of the literature of the 1970s. *AAHE Bulletin, 33,* 7–10.

Sullivan, A. M. (1977). A framework for the evaluation of teaching: Self-assessment and formal evaluation. In C. K. Knapper et al. (Eds.), *If teaching is important* [Canadian Association of University Teachers Monograph Series]. Published by: Clarke, Irwin.

Sykes, C. J. (1988). *ProfScam: Professors and the demise of higher education.* New York: St. Martin's Griffin.

Tapscott, D. (1996). *The digital economy: Promise and peril in the age of networked intelligence.* New York: McGraw-Hill.

Tarbox, E. (1996). *Everett Tarbox's statement on post tenure review* (pp. 1–3). Available: http://mama.indstate.edu/aaup/ej_ptr.html

Teachers Insurance and Annuity Association/College Retirement Equities Fund. (1997). *Hesburgh award winners.* New York: Author.

Teachers Insurance and Annuity Association/College Retirement Equities Fund. (1998). *Hesburgh award winners.* New York: Author.

Texas A & M University. (1998). *Rule on post-tenure review.* Texas A & M University, Faculty Senate. Retrieved from the World Wide Web July 7, 1998: http://www.tamu.edu/faculty_senate/post-tenure.html

Trower, C. A. (1996). Tenure snapshot. In *New pathways: Faculty careers and employment for the 21st century* (Vol. 2). Washington, DC: American Association for Higher Education.

University of Colorado at Denver. (1997, April 4). *Post tenure review.* Retrieved July 7, 1998, from the World Wide Web: http://www.cudenver.edu/public/affairs/Policies/Personnel/post tenure.html

University of Georgia. (1998, June 2). *Senior teaching fellows program.* Retrieved July 7, 1998, from the World Wide Web:

http://www.isd.uga.edu/Faculty%20Development/Teaching%20F
ellows.html#anchor26600468

University of Minnesota Graduate School. (1998, June 1).
Distinguished McKnight university professorship program.
Retrieved July 6, 1998, from the World Wide Web:
http://www.grad.umn.edu/grad/fellowships/mcknight.html

University of Nebraska–Omaha. (1998, June 30). *Center for faculty
development.* Retrieved July 12, 1998, from http://cid. unom-
aha.edu/~wwwcfd/index.html

University of Oregon. (1998). *Teaching circles: Teaching
effectiveness program.* Retrieved July 12, 1998, from
http://darkwing.uoregon.edu/~tep/library/articles/circles.html

University of Texas System. (1996, November 14). *Summary of
various post-tenure review policies.* Retrieved July 7, 1998, from
the World Wide Web:
http://www.utsystem.edu/News/exhibitc.htm

Vazulik, J. W., and Sullivan, R. L. (1986). *A faculty development
program in retrospect: Assessment and implications.* Paper
presented at Faculty Evaluation and Development: Lessons
Learned, Kansas City, MO.

Wadsworth, E. C. (Ed.). (1988). *A handbook for new practitioners.*
Stillwater, OK: New Forums Press.

Wilson, R. (1998, June 26). Provosts push a radical plan to change
the way faculty research is evaluated. *Chronicle of Higher
Education,* A12–A13.

Wise, D. (1995, October 30). Listserv discussion: heproc-faculty-
development@world.std.com. Retrieved July 13, 1998, from the
World Wide Web: http://www.rrpubs.com/heproc/ite/
msg00153.set5.shtml

Woodward, C. V. (1997). Academic freedom: An analysis of two
breaches. *Academic Questions, 10*(4), 71–74.

Wright, D. L. (1988). Program types and prototypes. In E. C.
Wadsworth (Ed.), *A handbook for new practitioners* (pp. 13–17).
Stillwater, OK: New Forums Press.

Wylie, N. R. (1990). A consortial approach: The Great Lakes
Colleges Association. In J. H. Schuster (Ed.), *Enhancing faculty
careers.* San Francisco: Jossey-Bass.

Zahorski, K. J. (1993). Taking the lead: Faculty development as
institutional change agent. *To Improve the Academy, 12,*
227–244.

INDEX

A

AACSB/EBI Management Education Faculty Study, 79–82, 92
Academic freedom, 3, 6, 7, 12
Adam, B. E., 73
Age of faculty members, 1, 4
Albright, M. J., 32
Aleamoni, L. M., 28, 41
Alstete, J. W., 15, 40, 46
Altman, H. B., 35, 69
Ambivalent faculty, 14
American Association of University Professors (AAUP), 8, 9, 12–13, 42
American University's retirement incentive program, 83–84
Andrews, H. A., 35, 56
Annual reviews, 10
Argyris, C., 24
Arnold, E. L., 24
ARNOLD© program, 55–56, 92–93
Assessment of faculty development programs, 79–83
Association of American Colleges (AAC), 8, 34
Atkins, S. S., 24
Attitudes of tenured professors, 17, 18
Austin, A. E., 72

B

Baez, B., 70
Baldridge, J. V., 45
Bannister, G., 1
Benchmarking, 46, 64
Bennett, J. B., 8, 11, 89
Bergquist, W. H., 4, 7, 25, 29, 32, 36, 37
Bernstein, G., 77
Blackburn, R. T., 25, 30
Bland, C. J., 1, 2, 4, 7, 28
Blum, D. E., 35
Boberg, A., 25
Boice, R., 41
Bowen, H. R., 5, 23
Bowman, M. A., 68
Boyer, E. L., 26
Braskamp, L. A., 28
Breneman, D. W., 2, 87
Brittain, A. W., 12
Brocato, J. J., 72
Broder, I., 83
Brooklyn College's Transformations program, 31, 46–48

Bush, A. G., 62
Bush Foundation, 27, 62–63
Business schools, 73–74

C

Career stages of faculty members, 22–23
Centra, J. A., 14, 25, 26, 29, 37, 39, 46, 70
Chabotar, K. J., 87
Chairs, key role of, 68
Chait, R., 3, 7
Chandler, J. B., 54
Chater S. S., 8, 11
Chesky, J., 42
Chism, N. V., 30, 70
Clark, S. M., 23, 27, 45, 88, 89
College of Charleston, 51
Conclusions on faculty development, 87–90
Conner, K. K., 76
Cook, P. J., 2
Corcoran, M. E., 23, 27
Cox, M. D., 48
Cramer, O., 12
Crawford, M., 21
Crawley, A., 19
Cullen, D. L., 41
Curtis, D. V., 45

D

Davies, P., 5
Definitions of faculty development, 32–35
Designing development programs: and assessment of programs, 79–83; budgeting tips on, 76; proposed model for, 65–66; recommendations and tools for, 66–79; and "weeding" of nondeveloping faculty, 83–85
Development programs: conclusions on, 87–90; defined, 32–35; history of, 25–32; jointly sponsored, 61–63; models of, 36–41, 65–66; need for, 14–19; optional, 46–57; and posttenure review, 41–44; required, 57–61; resources for, 91–95; sample guidelines for, 101–102. *See also* Designing development programs
Diamond, R. M., 38, 73
Distinguished McKnight University Professorship Program, 52–53
Ditwiler, E., 8

E

Eble, K. E., 15, 27, 30, 32, 46, 63
Ecker, G., 45
Educational Benchmarking Inc. (EBI), 79–82, 92

Effectiveness ratings, teacher, 14–15
Employment agreement, 4–5
Erickson, B. L., 30
Erikson, E., 22
Erickson, G. R., 30

F

Faculty, tenured: age of, 1, 4; attitudes characteristic of, 17, 18; development workshops led by, 76; and involvement in development activity, 26; and ownership of faculty development programs, 68–69; research production of, 7, 15, 16; retirement incentives for, 83–84; teaching circles for, 38, 77–78; teaching effectiveness of, 14–15

Faculty development: conclusions on, 87–90; defined, 32–35; history of, 25–32; jointly sponsored, 61–63; models of, 36–41, 65–66; need for, 14–19; optional, 46–57; and posttenure review, 41–44; required, 57–61; resources for, 91–95; sample guidelines for, 101–102. *See also* Designing development programs

Faculty Study, AACSB/EBI Management Education, 79–82, 92

Fantel, J. I., 6, 12

Farber, B. A., 17

Farmer, D. W., 56

Farr, G., 75, 76

Felicetti, D. A., 43

Finkelstein, M. J., 1, 15, 27, 67, 90

Formative evaluation, 10

Francis, J. B., 32

Frank, R. H., 2

Freedman, M., 30

French, J.R.P., 10

Funding for faculty development, 27, 51–55, 62–63

G

Gaff, J. G., 25, 30, 32, 36, 37, 41, 46

Geis, G. L., 10

Goodman, M. J., 12

Graf, D. L., 32, 33, 34, 89

Grid for mapping faculty development resources, 71–72

Growth contracts, 41

Guidelines for faculty development plan, 101–102

H

Hagan School of Business at Iona College, 75, 78, 80–82

Hagseth, J. A., 24

Hamilton, W. T., 69

Hammons, J. O., 70

Handbook for New Practitioners, A, 84

Literature search on faculty development, 2, 27–28, 29
Lovelace, B. E., 37
Lucas, A. F., 68
Luna, G., 41
Lunde, J. P., 42

M

Magner, D. K., 13
Malaise, 17, 18
Marginality, 17, 18
Martin, J. L., 6
Maslow, A., 21
Maslow's hierarchy of needs, 21
Mattering, 17, 18
Mbuh, R. N., 87
McCarthy, J., 6
McFerron, J. R., 34
McGregor, D., 21
McKeachie W. J., 15, 27, 30, 46, 63
Meaning, 17, 18
Mentoring by senior faculty, 40–41
Merit pay, 56
Metzger, W. P., 6
Meyer, H. H., 10
Miami University in Ohio, 48–50
Minimalist faculty, 14
Models of posttenure faculty development: current, 36–41; proposed model, 65–66
Moore, M. R., 68
Morreale, J. C., 5, 11, 13, 56, 68, 73, 74
Moscato, D., 68
Motivational factors, 21–22, 37–38

N

National Technological University, The, 87
Neal, J. E., 6, 13
Need for faculty development, 14–19
Nelson, W. C., 14, 30, 34, 46, 67, 68
NUPROF program, 54–55, 71, 97–99

O

O'Connell, W. R., 25
Olswang, S. G., 6, 12
Optional posttenure faculty development programs, 46–57
Organizational learning, 24
Ory, J. C., 28
Ownership of programs and activities, faculty's, 68–69

P

Panfor, S. C., 89

Parker, M. E., 14

Pellino, A., 25

Perley, J. E., 9

Phillips, S. R., 25, 29, 32, 36, 37

POD (Professional and Organizational Development)Network, 27, 30, 91

Postema, J., 63

Postle, D., 22

Posttenure developmentalism, 43

Posttenure faculty development: conclusions on, 87–90; defined, 32–35; history of, 25–32; jointly sponsored, 61–63; models of, 36–41, 65–66; need for, 14–19; optional, 46–57; and posttenure review, 41–44; required, 57–61; resources for, 91–95; sample guidelines for, 101–102. *See also* Designing development programs

Posttenure legalism, 43

Posttenure review: controversy over 8-9; for developmental purposes, 9–10, 12–13; five methods for, 10–11; and posttenure faculty development, 41–44; as self-analysis for professors, 13

Preedy, M., 89

R

Raufman, L., 78

Redditt, P. L., 69

Reisman, B., 8, 9, 10, 11, 42

Required posttenure faculty development, 57–61

Research production: on faculty development, 2, 27–28, 29; of tenured faculty, 7, 15, 16

Resources for faculty development, 91–95

Retirement age, uncapping of, 1, 12

Retirement incentives, 83–84

Review, posttenure. *See* Posttenure review

Rice, R. E., 13

Riches, C., 21

Rifkin, T., 3, 13, 41

Riley, G. L., 45

Rogers, C., 21

Rohrer, J. D., 72

Rubino, A. N., 72, 79

Rudolph, F., 3, 25

S

Sabbatical leaves: in current faculty development policies, 54, 55; and history of faculty development, 25, 28

Sample guidelines for faculty development plan, 101–102
Schmitz, C. C., 1, 2
Schön, D. A., 24
Schuster, J. H., 2, 5, 23, 90
Seal, R. K., 90
Self-directed faculty, 14
Sell, G. R., 30, 70
Senge, P. M., 24, 25, 87
Shapiro, H., 9
Siegel, M. E., 30, 34, 46, 67, 68
Smith, A., 2, 28, 30, 36, 89
Smith, P., 5
Sorcinelli, M. D., 68
Stordahl, B., 2, 32, 69, 70
Students, new breed of, 1, 19
Sullivan, A. M., 10, 68
Summative evaluation, 10
Sykes, C. J., 5

T

Tapscott, D.,1, 2, 87
Tarbox, E., 7
Teacher effectiveness ratings, 14–15
Teaching circles, 38, 77–78
Technology, new, 1, 2–3, 40
Tenure: and academic freedom, 3, 6, 7; alternatives to, 7; negative
    aspects of, 3; prevalence of, 3, 4; reasons for eliminating, 5;
    reasons for supporting, 7
Tenured professors: age of, 1, 4; attitudes characteristic of, 17, 18;
    development workshops led by, 76; and involvement in develop-
    ment activity, 26; and ownership of faculty development pro-
    grams, 68–69; research production of, 7, 15, 16; retirement incen-
    tives for, 83–84; teaching circles for, 38, 77–78; teaching
    effectiveness of, 14–15
Texas A&M University, 60
Theodore M. Hesburgh Award, 31, 46, 91
Theory X and Theory Y approach, 21, 44
TIAA-CREF, 31, 91
Trower, C. A., 3, 7
Twain, M., 4

U

University of Georgia Senior Teaching Fellows Program, 54, 71
University of Nebraska-Lincoln NUPROF program, 54–55, 71,
    97–99
University of Phoenix, 87

The mission of the Educational Resources Information Center (ERIC) system is to improve American education by increasing and facilitating the use of educational research and information on practice in the activities of learning, teaching, educational decision making, and research, wherever and whenever these activities take place.

Since 1983, the ASHE-ERIC Higher Education Report Series has been published in cooperation with the Association for the Study of Higher Education (ASHE). Starting in 2000, the series is published by Jossey-Bass in conjunction with the ERIC Clearinghouse on Higher Education.

Each monograph is the definitive analysis of a tough higher education problem, based on thorough research of pertinent literature and institutional experiences. Topics are identified by a national survey. Noted practitioners and scholars are then commissioned to write the reports, with experts providing critical reviews of each manuscript before publication.

Eight monographs (10 before 1985) in the ASHE-ERIC Higher Education Report series are published each year and are available on individual and subscription bases. To order, use the order form on the last page of this book.

Qualified persons interested in writing a monograph for the ASHE-ERIC Higher Education Report series are invited to submit a proposal to the National Advisory Board. As the preeminent literature review and issue analysis series in higher education, the Higher Education Reports are guaranteed wide dissemination and national exposure for accepted candidates. Execution of a monograph requires at least a minimal familiarity with the ERIC database, including *Resources in Education* and the current *Index to Journals in Education*. The objective of these reports is to bridge conventional wisdom with practical research.

ADVISORY BOARD

Susan Frost
Office of Institutional Planning and Research
Emory University

Kenneth Feldman
SUNY at Stony Brook

Anna Ortiz
Michigan State University

James Fairweather
Michigan State University

Lori White
Stanford University

Esther E. Gottlieb
West Virginia University

Carol Colbeck
Pennsylvania State University

Jeni Hart
University of Arizona

CONSULTING EDITORS

Martin Finkelstein
Seton Hall University

Mary Deane Sorcinelli
University of Massachusetts Amherst

Christine M. Licata
Rochester Institute of Technology

L. Dee Fink
The University of Oklahoma

Roseanna G. Ross
St. Cloud State University

REVIEW PANEL

John Centra
Syracuse University

Susan Frost
Emory University

James Palmer
Illinois State University

Sarah Dinham
University of Arizona

Harold Wechsler
University of Rochester

RECENT TITLES

Volume 27 ASHE-ERIC Higher Education Reports

1. The Art and Science of Classroom Assessment: The Missing Part of Pedagogy
   Susan M. Brookhart

2. Due Process and Higher Education: A Systemic Approach to Fair Decision Making
   Ed Stevens

3. Grading Students' Classroom Writing: Issues and Strategies
   Bruce W. Speck

Volume 26 ASHE-ERIC Higher Education Reports

1. Faculty Workload Studies: Perspectives, Needs, and Future Directions
   Katrina A. Meyer

2. Assessing Faculty Publication Productivity: Issues of Equity
   Elizabeth G. Creamer

3. Proclaiming and Sustaining Excellence: Assessment as a Faculty Role
   Karen Maitland Schilling and Karl L. Schilling

4. Creating Learning Centered Classrooms: What Does Learning Theory Have to Say?
   Frances K. Stage, Patricia A. Muller, Jillian Kinzie, and Ada Simmons

5. The Academic Administrator and the Law: What Every Dean and Department Chair Needs to Know
   J. Douglas Toma and Richard L. Palm

6. The Powerful Potential of Learning Communities: Improving Education for the Future
   Oscar T. Lenning and Larry H. Ebbers

7. Enrollment Management for the 21st Century: Institutional Goals, Accountability, and Fiscal Responsibility
   Garlene Penn

8. Enacting Diverse Learning Environments: Improving the Climate for Racial/Ethnic Diversity in Higher Education
   Sylvia Hurtado, Jeffrey Milem, Alma Clayton-Pedersen, and Walter Allen

Volume 25 ASHE-ERIC Higher Education Reports

1. A Culture for Academic Excellence: Implementing the Quality Principles in Higher Education
   Jann E. Freed, Marie R. Klugman, and Jonathan D. Fife

2. From Discipline to Development: Rethinking Student Conduct in Higher Education
   Michael Dannells

Back Issue/Subscription Order Form

Copy or detach and send to:
Jossey-Bass Inc., Publishers, 350 Sansome Street, San Francisco CA 94104-1342

Call or fax toll free!
Phone 888-378-2537 6AM-5PM PST; Fax 800-605-2665

Individual reports:	Please send me the following reports at $24 each
	(Important: please include series initials and issue number, such as AEHE 27:1)

1. AEHE _____

_____

_____

$ _____ Total for individual reports

$ _____ Shipping charges (for individual reports **only;** subscriptions are exempt from shipping charges): Up to $30, add $5^{50} • $30^{01}–$50, add $6^{50} $50^{01}–$75, add $8 • $75^{01}–$100, add $10 • $100^{01}–$150, add $12 Over $150, call for shipping charge

Subscriptions   Please ❏ start ❏ renew my subscription to *ASHE-ERIC Higher Education Reports* for the year <u>2000</u> at the following rate (8 issues):   U.S. $144   Canada: $169   All others: $174

Please ❏ start my subscription to *ASHE-ERIC Higher Education Reports* for the year <u>2001</u> at the following rate (6 issues): U.S. $108   Canada: $133   All others: $138

NOTE: Subscriptions are for the calendar year only. Subscriptions begin with Report 1 of the year indicated above.

$ _____ Total individual reports and subscriptions (Add appropriate sales tax for your state for individual reports. No sales tax on U.S. subscriptions. Canadian residents, add GST for subscriptions and individual reports.)

❏ Payment enclosed (U.S. check or money order only)
❏ VISA, MC, AmEx, Discover Card # _____ Exp. date _____

Signature _____ Day phone _____
❏ Bill me (U.S. institutional orders only. Purchase order required)
Purchase order #_____
Federal Tax ID 135593032   GST 89102-8052

Name _____
Address _____

Phone_____ E-mail _____

For more information about Jossey-Bass Publishers, visit our Web site at:
www.josseybass.com   **PRIORITY CODE = ND1**